John Robert Hutchinson

The Quest of the Golden Pearl

John Robert Hutchinson

The Quest of the Golden Pearl

ISBN/EAN: 9783743313385

Manufactured in Europe, USA, Canada, Australia, Japa

Cover: Foto ©ninafisch / pixelio.de

Manufactured and distributed by brebook publishing software (www.brebook.com)

John Robert Hutchinson

The Quest of the Golden Pearl

THE QUEST
OF THE GOLDEN PEARL

BY

J. R. HUTCHINSON

AUTHOR OF "'WAY DOWN EAST," "HAL HUNGERFORD," ETC.

WITH ILLUSTRATIONS BY

HUME NISBET

London

WARD AND DOWNEY
LIMITED

12 YORK BUILDINGS ADELPHI W.C.

1897

[All rights reserved]

F. M. EVANS AND CO., LIMITED, PRINTERS,
CRYSTAL PALACE, S.E.

CONTENTS.

CHAPTER I.
THE SHARK-CHARMER WALKS THE PLANK 1

CHAPTER II.
A STROKE OF LUCK AND AN AFTER-STROKE 10

CHAPTER III.
THE QUEST BEGINS 20

CHAPTER IV.
INTRODUCES DOSIN, AND TELLS HOW CAPTAIN MANGO PROVED HIMSELF A TRUMP 37

CHAPTER V.
THE LASCAR GETS HIS KNIFE BACK 5

CHAPTER VI.
IN THE THICK OF IT 69

CHAPTER VII.
" FUN OR FIGHTING, I'M READY, ANYHOW!" . . . 87

CHAPTER VIII.

AT THE HAUNTED PAGODAS 102

CHAPTER IX.

WAS IT JACK? 118

CHAPTER X.

IN WHICH THE OLD SAW, "OUT OF THE FRYING-PAN, INTO THE FIRE," IS REVERSED WITH STARTLING EFFECT . . 132

CHAPTER XI.

INTO THE HEART OF THE HILL 141

CHAPTER XII.

RELATES HOW A WRONG ROAD LED TO THE RIGHT PLACE . 149

CHAPTER XIII.

CAPTAIN MANGO "GOES ALOFT" 155

CHAPTER XIV.

SHROUDED IN A HAMMOCK 167

CHAPTER XV.

THE CROCODILE PIT 177

CHAPTER XVI.

DON SETS A DEATH-TRAP FOR THE LASCAR 184

CHAPTER XVII.

THE BLAST OF A CONCH-SHELL 189

CONTENTS.

CHAPTER XVIII.
BETWEEN LIFE AND DEATH 199

CHAPTER XIX.
ONE-TO-TWENTY GIVES TWENTY-TO-ONE THE WORST OF IT . 210

CHAPTER XX.
THE LAST STRAW 217

CHAPTER XXI.
RIVALS FOR THE HONOURS OF DEATH 234

CHAPTER XXII.
A REPORT FROM THE SEA 242

CHAPTER XXIII.
DON RUNS THE GAUNTLET 251

CHAPTER XXIV.
IN THE NICK OF TIME 259

CHAPTER XXV.
THE SHARK-CHARMER IS CAUGHT IN HIS OWN TRAP . . 267

CHAPTER XXVI.
BRINGS THE QUEST TO AN END 272

LIST OF ILLUSTRATIONS.

	PAGE
THE HAUNTED PAGODAS	*Frontispiece*
THE SHARK-CHARMER	8
THE EMPTY LOCKER	17
THE VISIT TO CAPTAIN MANGO	43
THE LASCAR LAUNCHES THE BALLAM	*facing* 52
BECALMED IN THE MOONLIGHT	*facing* 57
IN THE TEMPLE	81
THE EXPLOSION	125
DON AND THE SENTINEL	195
THE CROCODILE PIT	205
DON GOES DOWN THE CLIFF	*facing* 248

THE QUEST OF THE GOLDEN PEARL.

CHAPTER I.

THE SHARK-CHARMER WALKS THE PLANK.

"Jack! I say, Jack! there's a row among the boatmen."

A sturdy, thick-set young fellow of seventeen was Jack, with low-hung fists of formidable size, and a love for anything in the shape of a row that constantly led him into scrapes. Hot-headed though he was, he was one of the most good-humoured, well-meaning young fellows in the world, who, while he would not hurt a fly if he could help it, was always ready to fight in defence of his own or another's rights.

His chum, Roydon Leigh—"Don" for short—was of an altogether different type of young manhood. Jack's senior by a year, he was tall for his age, standing five feet ten in his stockings. His lithe, wiry frame contrasted strongly with Jack's sturdier build, as did his Scotch "canniness" with that young gentleman's headlong impetuosity.

"A row!" cried Jack delightedly, as he rushed to the taffrail. "Time, too; four weeks we've lain here, and never a hand in a single shindy!"

His companion laughed.

"As for that," said he, "you're not likely to have a hand in this, unless you take the boat and row off to the diving grounds. All the same, there's a jolly row on—look yonder."

The schooner *Wellington* rode at anchor at the northern extremity of the Strait of Manaar, on the famous pearl-fishing grounds of Ceylon. On her larboard bow lay the coast—a string of low, white sand-hills, dotted with the dark-brown thatch of fisher huts and the vivid green of cocoa-nut palms. The hour was eight o'clock in the morning of a cloudless March day; the fitful land-breeze had died away, leaving the whole surface of the sea like billowy glass. Half-a-dozen cable's-lengths distant on the schooner's starboard quarter, a score or more of native *dhonies* or diving-boats rose and dipped to the regular motion of the long groundswell.

It was towards these boats that Don pointed.

That something unusual had occurred was evident enough. Angry shouts floated across the placid water; and the native boatmen could be seen hurriedly pulling the boats together into a compact group about one central spot where the clamour was loudest.

"I say," cried Jack, after watching the boats for some time in silence, "they're making for the schooner."

"I don't half like the look of it," replied Don uneasily; "they shouldn't leave the diving grounds, you know, until the signal gun's fired. I wish the guv was here."

"Wishing's no good when he's ashore," said Jack philosophically. "You're the skipper *pro tem.*, and you must make the most of your promotion, old fellow. We'll have some fun, anyhow. Whew! how those niggers pull, and what a jolly row they're making!"

By this time the excited cries, which had first attracted the attention of those upon the schooner's deck, had been exchanged by the boatmen for a weird chant, to which every oar kept time. Erect in the stern of the foremost boat an old whiteheaded *tyndal* or "master" led the song, while at the end of each measure a hundred voices raised a chorus that seemed fairly to lift the boats clear of the water.

"What are they singing, anyway?" demanded Jack. "There's something about a diver and a shark in it, but I can't half make it out, can you?"

"We'll call Puggles—he'll be able to tell us. Pug! Hi, Pug! come here."

"Coming, sa'b!" answered a voice from the cook's galley; and almost simultaneously there appeared on deck the plumpest, shiniest, most good-natured looking black boy that ever displayed two rows of pearly teeth. Nature had, apparently, pulled him into the world by the nose, and then, as a sort of finishing touch to the job, had given that organ a sharp upward tweak and left it so. It was to this feature that Puggles owed his name.

"Pug," said his master, "tell us what those boatmen yonder are singing."

The black boy cocked his ears and listened for a moment with parted lips. "Boat-wallahs this way telling, sa'b," said he; and, catching the strain of the chant, he repeated the words of each line as it fell from the lips of the old *tyndal*:

> Salambo selling the diver one charm,
> Salaam, Alli kum!
> Old shark, he telling, then do no harm,
> Salaam, Alli kum!

One spotted shark come out the south,
 Salaam, Alli kum!
He taking diver's leg in his mouth,
 Salaam, Alli kum!
Me big liking got, he telling, for you,
 Salaam, Alli kum!
So he biting diver clean in two,
 Salaam, Alli kum!
The lying charmer we take to the ship,
 Salaam, Alli kum!
There he feeling bite of the sahib's whip,
 Salaam, Alli kum!

"Why, this Salambo must be the chap the guv had whipped off the grounds last season, eh, Pug?" cried Don excitedly.

"Same black rascal, sa'b. His skin getting well, he coming back. Dey bring him 'board ship, make his skin sore two times," explained Puggles, grinning.

"Ha, ha!" laughed Jack. "We'll oblige 'em! We'll trice the fellow up! Hullo, here they come!"

The boats having now reached the schooner, the chant ceased abruptly, the heavy oars were noisily shipped, and, amid a perfect Babel of voices, the boatmen came swarming up the sides, until the deck was one mass of wildly gesticulating, dusky humanity. The uproar was terrific.

The old *tyndal*, who towered a full head and

shoulders above his comrades, pushed his way to the front, and commanding silence among his followers, addressed himself to Don, who was always recognised as master in his father's absence.

"Sa'b," said he in pigeon English, "one year back big sa'b ordering Salambo eat plenty blows for selling charm to diver-man. All same, this season he done come back and sell plenty charm, telling diver-man he put charm round neck, shark no eat him up. He telling plenty lie—this morning one shark done come, eat diver, charm, all!"

"Let him stand forward," said Don, beginning to enter as much into the novelty of the thing as Jack himself.

The culprit, a sleek old fellow with shaven head, crafty eyes, and a rosary of wooden beads about his neck, was shoved to the front.

"Are you the chap who was whipped off the grounds last year for selling charms?" demanded Don.

"Your honour speaking true words," whined the shark-charmer, salaaming until his shaven head almost touched the deck; "I same rascal."

"I say, Jack," whispered Don, "I shan't have him whipped, you know. We'll make him walk the plank."

"Capital! He'll funk, certain, and there'll be no end of fun."

"We'll do it, then," said Don decidedly. "Go forward and order two of the lascars to take the boat and lie under the schooner's quarter—this side, you know—ready to pick him up."

In high glee Jack departed to execute this commission, while Don again turned to the shark-doctor.

"Do you happen to have one of those charms about you?" he asked.

"One here got, sa'b," said the fellow, producing from the folds of his waist-cloth an *ola* or fragment of palm-leaf, covered with cabalistic characters. "Sa'b no look at him?"

"Keep it yourself," said Don; "you'll soon need it. Hi, lascar!" to one of the schooner's crew who stood near. "Fetch a plank here and run it out over the side."

By the time the plank was brought and run out until one-half its length projected over the water, Jack came up chuckling, and by a sign intimated that the boat was in readiness. The crowd of natives, guessing that something unusual was afoot, craned their necks eagerly, while Puggles executed a comic *pas seul* in his delight. But the shark-charmer, as Jack had predicted, "funked" miserably.

Knowing that with the boat in waiting there was absolutely no danger to the shark-charmer's life, Don turned a deaf ear to his pleadings, and made a signal to the lascars to proceed.

THE SHARK-CHARMER.

Willing hands seized the quaking wretch and dragged him to the schooner's side, where he was placed upon the plank, Puggles standing on the deck-end to keep it down.

"Steady, Puggles!" cried Don. "One, two, three—let him slide!"

Puggles jumped aside, the deck-end of the plank rose high in air, then descended with a crash; and with a scream of terror the shark-charmer disappeared over the side.

A tremendous shout rose from the natives on deck, and with a common impulse they one and all rushed to the schooner's side, which they reached just as the shark-charmer's head reappeared above the surface. Another moment, and he was dragged into the boat, where, catching sight of the laughing faces ranged along the rail above, he shook his fist in mute menace, and so was rowed to shore.

"Teach the beggar a lesson he won't forget in a hurry," said Don, as he watched the boat recede. "Good-bye, old boy; we're not likely to meet again."

But in this sanguine forecast of the future he was mistaken, as events speedily proved.

CHAPTER II.

A STROKE OF LUCK AND AN AFTER-STROKE.

It was the afternoon of the day on which the shark-charmer so unwillingly walked the plank. The breeze was so light and fitful that it barely ruffled the surface of the sea about the schooner. Weary of the narrow limits of the deck, Don and his chum dropped into the boat and rowed ashore —Puggles, as a matter of course, bearing them company.

"These beastly sands are like an oven!" growled Don, lifting his helmet to cool his dripping forehead. "Where shall we go, Jack?"

"Bazaar," replied Jack laconically; "always some fun to be had there. Pug, point for the bazaar."

"Me pointing, sar," puffed the black boy, setting his dumpy legs in motion.

Puggles was never so much in his element as

when thus strutting pompously in advance, warning common nigger humanity of the white sahibs' approach. At such times the disdainful tilt of his nose, the supreme self-complaisance of his expansive grin, were as good as a show.

A gay and animated scene did the bazaar present. Back and forth through the temporary street surged an endless throng of natives of every shade of complexion and variety of costume—buying, selling, shouting, jabbering, drinking with friends or fighting with enemies.

"Much cry and little wool," laughed Jack. "There's a big black fellow yonder auctioning off some pearl oysters; let's have a go at the next lot."

"All right," assented Don; "perhaps we'll have a stroke of luck. The guv knew a poor half-caste once who bid in just such a chance lot as this, and in one of them he found sixty-eight thumping big pearls. Cleared thousands of pounds by that one bid, the guv says. Pug! here, Pug!"

"Coming, sa'b," gasped a faint voice, and Puggles wriggled his way from amongst the bystanders, shining with abundant perspiration, and squeezed well-nigh flat by the pressure of the crowd.

"Pug," said his master, "up on this creel with you, and when that big black fellow yonder puts up his next lot, bid 'em in."

Up went Puggles, nothing loth to escape further squeezing, and up went the auctioneer's next lot. In five minutes' time the few dozens of oysters composing the lot were knocked down to the black boy at an absurdly low figure.

"Here you are," said Don, handing him the coin. "Pass that over, and fetch the things away till we see what's inside them."

Making a dive for the oysters, Puggles scrambled them into his cloth, and followed the sahibs to the outskirts of the crowd, blowing like a porpoise. Finding a convenient patch of shade beneath a banyan tree within a few yards of the lazy surf, they proceeded to ascertain, without further delay, whether the shells contained anything of value.

"Him plenty smell got, anyhow," commented Puggles, as he arranged the oysters, which had been several days out of the water, in a small pyramid.

Jack threw himself on the sand, and surveyed the rough, discoloured heap with unqualified disgust. "They don't look very promising, I must say," he cried. "Try that big one on top, Don."

Inserting the blade of his pocket-knife between the shells of the bivalve, Don prized it open and carefully examined its contents. It contained nothing of any value.

Jack looked listlessly on, while his companion opened shell after shell with no other result than the finding of two or three miserable specimens of pearls, so small that, as Jack laughingly said, "one might stick them in one's eye and forget the moment after where one had put them."

Only three or four shells now remained unopened, and Don was on the point of abandoning the search in disgust, when Jack, who had edged himself on his elbow as close to the heap as the villainous odour of the decomposed oysters would allow, snatched up a shell of large size, and said:

"Let me have the knife a moment, will you? This looks promising—it's the biggest of the whole lot, anyhow."

"There you are, then; I've had enough of them myself," said Don, tossing him the knife and walking off.

He had not proceeded half-a-dozen yards, however, when a loud shout brought him back at a run. Jack and Puggles were eagerly bending over the opened oyster.

"What is it?" he asked breathlessly, going down on his knees beside them.

Jack thrust the half-shell towards him. It was literally filled with magnificent pearls.*

Not a word was spoken as the glistening, priceless globules were carefully abstracted from their unsightly case and laid upon Pug's coffee-coloured palm. Twenty-five pearls of matchless size and brilliancy did Jack count out ere the store was exhausted. So taken up were they with their good fortune that not one of the three observed a native creep stealthily towards them under cover of the tree.

"There's been nothing like it known on the grounds for years!" cried Don excitedly. "Any more, Jack?"

"No more," said Jack, and was about to throw the shell away, when Puggles caught his arm.

"Stop, sar, stop! Me see something yellow in shell. Stick knife in the meat, sar, that side."

With the point of the blade Jack prodded the substance of the oyster at the point indicated, and presently laid bare the queen of the royal family of pearls on which they had stumbled. Larger

---

* In 1828 no less than sixty-seven pearls were taken from a single oyster on these grounds.—J. R. H.

by far than any of the twenty-five already taken from the shell, this latest addition to the number was in shape like a pear, in lustre of the purest pale yellow.

"Him gold pearl, sa'b!" cried Puggles gleefully, grinning from ear to ear. "Other only silver. Gold pearl plenty price fetching."

"Jack, old fellow," cried Don, thumping his companion on the back, "Puggles is right; we're in luck. I've heard the guv say that a golden pearl isn't found once in twenty years. The priests are ready to give simply any sum you like for a really fine specimen."

The native who had concealed himself behind the trunk of the banyan tree, leaned eagerly forward. So close was he to the absorbed group that he could distinctly hear every word of their conversation. As he listened, an avaricious glitter shone in his crafty eyes, and he rubbed his hands unctuously together, as though he were rubbing pearls between them.

"How much do you suppose the lot is worth, Don?" Jack inquired.

"Some thousands of pounds, I should say. But the guv will be able to tell us. Say, I'd better put them in this."

Taking out his watch, he drew off the soft chamois leather case, and carefully transferred the output of the mammoth oyster from Pug's palm to this temporary receptacle.

"Now," cried Jack, leaping to his feet, "let's make for the schooner. The sun's set, and besides, I shan't feel easy until the golden 'un is in a safer place than a waistcoat pocket."

"That's so," assented Don. "Point, Pug!"

When they had disappeared in the crowded bazaar, the shark-charmer emerged from behind the tree, and took the road to that part of the beach where the boats lay.

By the time Don and his companions reached the schooner, the brief twilight had deepened into the gray darkness of early night. The pearls were at once shown to Captain Leigh, who confirmed his son's estimate of their value. It would, he said, run well into four figures, if not into five. The golden pearl he pronounced to be of special value.

"Not that it would fetch anything in England," said he; "but wealthy natives—and more especially priests—stop at nothing to secure a pearl like that. I mean that in a double sense, my lads; so you had better stow your find away in a safe place."

"I shall put it in the little locker under the cabin clock," said Don. "It locks, and there isn't a safer place on board the schooner."

THE EMPTY LOCKER.

In the locker under the cabin clock, accordingly, the chamois leather bag with its precious contents was placed. On closing the locker, however, to his annoyance Don found the key to be missing.

"Wrap your handkerchief round the bag, so it won't be noticed if any one opens the locker," suggested Jack. "It will be safe enough then, especially as nobody ever comes here except ourselves and Pug."

But on quitting the cabin, to their amazement they came face to face with the shark-charmer! He stood at the very bottom of the companion-way, within a yard of the cabin door, and directly opposite the clock and locker.

"What are you doing here?" cried Don, advancing upon him angrily.

"Nothing, sa'b, nothing!" protested the native, dropping a running salvo of salaams as he backed up the steps. "Me only wanting to see big sa'b."

"Then be off about your business, or you'll get the whipping you missed this morning. Do you hear?" And, without further ado, Salambo made for the deck, where they saw him disappear over the side.

"Do you think he saw us at the locker, Jack?" Don asked uneasily.

"I should think not. But even if he did he wouldn't be any the wiser. He knows nothing about the pearls."

"True enough," said Don, and so the subject dropped.

The cabin clock indicated the hour of ten when they turned in for the night. Somehow Don found himself unable to sleep. In spite of every effort he could make to the contrary, his thoughts *would* run on the pearls. At last he could stand it no longer. Leaping out of his berth, he struck a light and crept noiselessly into the main cabin. The companion door stood open to admit the night air, and his candle flared in the draught.

"I'll get to sleep, perhaps, if I take a look at them," he said to himself as he made his way to the locker.

An exclamation of alarm burst from his lips. His hand shook so violently that it was with difficulty he could hold the candle. The lid of the locker stood wide open!

Advancing the light, he peered into the receptacle. It contained nothing. Handkerchief, bag, pearls—all had disappeared!

CHAPTER III.

THE QUEST BEGINS.

For a moment the discovery paralysed him, body and mind. Then he turned and hurried to Jack's cabin. Jack was snoring. Don shook him fiercely by the shoulder.

"Wake up! The pearls are gone!"

Jack was awake and on his feet in a twinkling. "You're dreaming, old fellow," said he, seeing Don in his night-clothes. "You're only half awake."

Don did not argue the matter. He simply seized Jack by the arm and dragged him into the main cabin. There the empty locker placed the truth of his assertion beyond dispute.

"What's to be done?" gasped Jack.

"Let us call Pug," suggested Don. "He may know something about this."

Puggles slept on deck. In two minutes they were by his side, and he was stretching his jaws in a mighty yawn. Great was his astonishment when he heard of the loss. But he could throw no light on the matter. He had neither seen nor heard anything suspicious. As for Puggles himself, he was above suspicion.

"Come down and let us have another look," said Jack. "It's just possible, you know, that some one may have been to the locker and accidentally dropped or knocked the case out upon the floor. I can't believe it's gone."

Just as they reached the bottom of the companion-way, Puggles, who was slightly in advance of his master, stopped short, and called their attention to an object dangling from the handle of the door. Jack caught it up and ran to the table, where the lighted candle stood.

"Merely a string of wooden beads," said he, tossing the object on the table.

"A native rosary!" cried Don, snatching it up. "I've seen this before somewhere."

"Sa'b," broke in Puggles, his eyes the size and colour of Spanish onions, "him shark-charmer rosilly, sa'b!"

"The very same!" cried Don. "I recollect seeing it round his neck this morning."

"And I recollect seeing it there this evening," added Jack.

"When we bundled him out of the companion-way?"

"Yes."

"Then how do you account for our finding it on the door-knob, and for its being broken as it is now?"

"Don't you see? The fellow returned, of course."

"Returned? When?"

"After we saw him over the side; he never went ashore. He sneaked back, and then made off in a tremendous hurry. The position, not to say the condition, in which we found the rosary proves that. Jove! what a pair of fools we've been. That rascally shark-charmer has diddled us out of the pearls."

Don stared at his friend open-mouthed, yet unable to utter a single word either of assent or doubt, so great was the consternation produced in his mind by Jack's daring theory as to the disappearance of the pearls, and the consequences which must follow if it held good.

"You may take it to be a dead certainty,' resumed Jack, following up his idea, "that when Salambo actually left the ship, the pearls went with him. We made the rascal walk the plank this morning, and he's bound to resent that, of course. In fact, the way in which he shook his fist at us when he went off in the boat shows that he *did* resent it. Very well, then, there's a ready-made motive for you—revenge."

"That's all right," said Don, finding his tongue at last, "I'm not boggling over the motive: the value of the pearls is enough motive for any nigger. What puzzles me is this: How did he know we had them in our possession at all?"

"Why, that's as plain as the nose on your face," replied Jack; "the fellow was on shore at the same time we were, was he not?"

"He was."

"Well, then, suppose he saw us buy the shells, watched us open them, and, in short, discovered that we had met with a stroke of luck. Then he follows us back here—you saw him yourself, didn't you?"

"I did," said Don.

"And you see this, don't you?" dangling the rosary before Don's eyes.

"I do; I'm not blind."

"Then what the dickens more do you want?"

"The pearls," said Don, laughing. "I'm convinced, old fellow, so no more palaver. Our business now is to run the shark-charmer down. What's the time?"

"Eleven o'clock to the minute."

"And what start of us do you think he has got?"

"It was about nine when we caught him sneaking, and we turned in at ten."

"And out again half an hour later. Then the locker must have been rifled between ten and half-past. That would give him, say, forty-five minutes' start if we were on his track at this identical moment, which we—— What was that? I heard a noise overhead."

"Some one at the skylight," said Jack in a whisper. "S-s-sh! I'll slip on deck and see who it is."

The skylight referred to was situated directly over the cabin table, so that, its sash being then raised some six inches to admit the night air, it afforded a ready means of eavesdropping. Springing lightly up the cabin steps in his stocking feet, Jack took a cautious survey of the deck. The awning had been taken in at nightfall, and a full moon shone overhead, making the whole deck as light as day. Close beside the skylight, lashed against the cabin, stood a water-butt; and bending carelessly over this he saw one of the native crew. Calling out sharply, he bade him go forward, and the fellow, muttering some half-audible excuse about wanting a drink, slunk away.

"A lascar after water; I don't think he was spying," said Jack, diving below again. "All the same, we'll keep an eye aloft; that rascally Salambo may have an accomplice among the crew."

"Very likely; but as I was saying," resumed Don, in a lower key, "the thief has had ample time to make himself scarce. Now the thing is—how are we to nab him?"

"There are the *peons*.* Why not get the guv to set them on the fellow's track?"

"Why, there's just the difficulty," said Don, with a despairing gesture. "They all sleep ashore except one or two; and by the time we woke the governor, explained matters to him, and got the fellows started, there'd be no end of delay. Besides, the rascal would naturally be on the look-out for the *peons*, and either give them the slip or bribe them to let him off."

"That's so; whatever's done must be done sharp."

"Just what I was going to say," continued

* Native attendants; pronounced *pewns*.—J..R. H.

Don. "The schooner, you see, sails for Colombo in two or three days' time at the most, and it would put the governor to no end of inconvenience to despatch half-a-dozen *peons* on an errand like this just now. Fact is, I doubt if he'd do it at all, and we might go whistle for our pearls. No, I've a better plan than that to propose. There's no need to trouble the guv at all; we'll go ashore and capture the thief ourselves."

"Capital!" cried Jack; "I'd like nothing better. When shall we start?"

"At once. There's a bright moon, the fellow has only about an hour's start, and with ordinary luck we ought to run him down by daybreak at the very——"

"Hist!" said Jack suddenly; "there's some one at the skylight again. Wait a minute—I'll soon put an end to his spying."

Clearing the ladder at a bound, he emerged upon the deck before the listener was aware of his approach. The spy was actually bending over the open skylight. He was there for no good or friendly purpose—that was evident.

"You're not after water this time, anyhow," said Jack, hauling him off the cabin with scant ceremony. "Didn't I tell you to go forward?

You'll obey orders next time, perhaps;" and drawing off, he felled him to the deck with a single blow.

The lascar picked himself up and scuttled forward, muttering curses beneath his breath.

"There," said Jack quietly, as he rejoined those below, "we'll not be spied upon again to-night, I fancy. Now, Don, for the rest of your plan."

"That's soon told. I propose that we follow the thief at once. The only difficulty will be to get on his track."

"Marster going take me?" queried Puggles anxiously.

"Why, of course," said Don; "we couldn't manage without you, Pug."

"Then," said Puggles, grinning, "me soon putting on track; me knowing place Salambo sleeping plenty nights."

"Good; there's something in that," said Don. "He is sure to go straight to his den on leaving the schooner, though it's hardly likely he'll remain there to sleep. Still, he might. 'Twill give us a clue to his whereabouts, at all events. And now, Jack, ready's the word."

No time was to be lost, and quietly and quickly their preparations were completed. These were by no means extensive : they fully expected to return to the schooner by break of day. A revolver, half-a-dozen rounds of ammunition, and a few rupees disposed in their pockets, they stole noiselessly on deck. The night was one of breathless calm, and the watch lay stretched upon their backs, snoring away the sultry hours of duty. Save our three adventurers, not a living thing was astir; not a sound broke the stillness of the night; and high overhead the moon floated in ghostly splendour.

The boat, as it chanced, lay on that side of the schooner farthest from the shore; and in order to shape their course for the beach it was necessary to round the vessel's bows. Puggles held the tiller-ropes, but in doing this he miscalculated his distance, and ran the boat full tilt against the schooner's cable.

"Keep her off, Pug!" cried his master in suppressed, half-angry tones. "Can't you see where you're steering?"

In the momentary confusion a figure appeared for a moment above the schooner's bulwarks. Then a glittering object hurtled through the moonlit air and struck the gun'le of the boat immediately abaft the thwart on which Jack sat. Jack uttered a stifled cry and dropped his oar.

"What's the matter?" said Don impatiently, as the boat swung clear of the cable. "Pull, old fellow; we've no time to lose."

"Better lose a little time than one's life," muttered Jack through his set teeth. "Look here!"

Turning in his seat Don saw, still quivering in the gun'le of the boat where its point had stuck, a sailor's heavy sheath-knife. In its passage it had slashed open the shoulder of Jack's coat, grazing the flesh so closely as to draw blood—the first shed in the quest of the golden pearl.

Jack passed it off with an air of indifference.

"A mere scratch," said he; "but a close shave all the same. The work of that treacherous lascar I knocked down a while back. Saw his ugly head-piece above the rail just now, don't you know. There's no time to pay him out now, but if ever he interferes with me again he'll get his knife back, anyhow!" and wrenching the formidable weapon free of the plank, he thrust it into his belt and again bent to his oar.

"If that fellow's an accomplice of the shark-charmer, it looks as though they meant business," commented Don, seconding his companion's stroke.

"So do we, if it comes to that," was Jack's significant retort.

For some time they pulled in silence, the creaking of the oars in the rowlocks and the soft purling of the water about the boat's prow being the only sounds audible. When within a couple of hundred yards of the gleaming surf-line, Don suddenly broke the silence.

"Hold hard, Jack! Do you make out anything astern there — anything black on the water?"

"Nothing," said Jack, after a moment's hesitation.

"It's gone now, but I saw it quite plainly. Struck me it looked like a man's head. Must have been a dugong."

"Or the lascar," suggested Jack. "He's safe to follow us if he's an accomplice."

"Hardly safe with so many sharks about," rejoined Don, "unless his master has provided him with an extra potent charm."

Five minutes later, the boat having meanwhile been beached upon the deserted sands, Puggles was rapidly "pointing" for the bazaar, where the shark-charmer slept o' nights. That they should find him there to-night, however, was almost too much to hope. He had probably "made tracks" with all speed after securing the pearls. All the same, a visit to the bazaar might furnish some clue to his present whereabouts.

"Stop!" said Don, when within fifty yards of the spot. "The whole place will be astir in two minutes if we show ourselves, Jack. We'd better send Pug on ahead to reconnoitre while we wait here. Do you know the hut he usually sleeps in, Pug?"

"Me finding with me eyes shut, sa'b."

"Good! Now listen. Make your way to this hut as quietly as you can, and ascertain whether he's there or not. If he's there, don't wake him, but come back here as fast as your legs can carry you. If he's not there, try and find out where he's gone."

"Put your cloth over your head so he won't recognise you, and say you've come on business," put in Jack. "Pretend you want a charm, or something of that sort."

"Not a bad idea," assented Don. "You understand, Pug?"

"Me understanding, sa'b."

"Then be off with you, sharp!"

Puggles promptly disappeared.

In the course of ten minutes he returned, accompanied by a native muffled from head to heel in a blanket.

"Surely he can't have induced the old fellow to return with him!" whispered Jack excitedly.

But in this surmise he was wrong. It was not the shark-charmer.

"Dis one bery nice black man; plenty talk got," said Puggles, by way of introduction, when he reached the spot where his master and Jack were waiting. "Him telling shark-charmer no here; he going one village."

"Just as I feared," said Don. "How far is it to this village, Pug?"

"Him telling one two legs," replied Puggles, meaning leagues. "Village 'long shore; marster giving one rupee, dis black man showing way."

Without further parley the rupee was transferred from Don's pocket to the stranger's outstretched palm, and off they started. After following the beach for about a mile, their guide turned his back upon the sea and struck inland, leading them a tortuous course amid ghostly, interminable sand-hills, where the mournful sighing of the night-wind through the tall silver-grass, and the howling of predatory jackals, added to the weird loneliness of the scene. A blurred furrow in the yielding sand formed the only footpath. So slow was their progress that when at last the guide pointed out the village a half-mile ahead, Don, on consulting his watch, found it to be three o'clock. They had wasted fully two hours in walking six miles.

While they were still some little distance short of the village, the guide stopped, and pointing out a pool of water which shone like a boss of polished silver amid the sand-hills, asked leave to go and slake his thirst. His request granted, he disappeared amid the dunes.

"Do you know," said Jack, while they were impatiently awaiting his return, "I fancy I've seen that fellow before, though I can't for the life of me recall where."

The guide not returning, they at length went in search of him. But Pug's "bery nice black man" was nowhere to be seen.

"Looks as if he meant to leave us in the lurch," Jack began, when a shout of "Him here got, sa'b!" from Puggles, brought them back to the footpath at a run.

The new-comer, however, was not the missing guide, but a stranger. He had been belated at the bazaar, he told them, and was now making his way home to the village close by. In answer to inquiries concerning the shark-charmer, he imparted a startling piece of news.

The shark-charmer had indeed taken his departure from the bazaar, but not to this village. He had, the stranger asserted, embarked in a coasting vessel bound for the opposite side of the Strait.

Don uttered an exclamation of impatience and dismay.

"He will be safe on the Madras coast by daybreak!" he cried.

"Him there coming from, sa'b," put in Puggles.

"And that lying guide," added Jack savagely, "was an accomplice, left behind to throw us off the scent. Don't you remember you saw some one swimming after the boat? I'll lay any odds 'twas the lascar. He got to the bazaar ahead of us—he could easily manage that, you know, by running along the sands — muffled himself up so that I shouldn't recognise him, and then led us on this fool's errand while his master made off. Well, good-bye to the golden 'un!"

"Not a bit of it!" cried Don resolutely. "I, for one, shan't relinquish the quest, come what may. Back we go to the schooner! Then, with the governor's consent, we'll go further. Point, Pug!"

Jack seconding this proposal heartily, they rewarded the communicative native, and with unflagging determination retraced their steps. By four o'clock they had traversed something more than half the distance. The dawn star was now high above the eastern horizon. A rosy flush in the same quarter warned them that day was rapidly approaching. Suddenly, out of the gray distance ahead, a dull booming sound floated to their ears.

"The schooner's signal gun!" exclaimed Don. "Why, it's too early yet by a good hour for the boats to put out. What's the governor about, I wonder?"

"There it goes again!" cried Jack. "I never knew it to be fired twice of a morning, did you?"

"Never," said Don uneasily. "Come, let us get on!"

Off again at their best speed, until at length the heavy path was exchanged for the smooth, hard sand of the beach. On this it was possible to make better time, and by five o'clock they were within half a mile or so of the bazaar. It was now daylight; but a sharp bend in the coast-line, and the sand-hills which here rose steeply from the beach on their left, as yet concealed both the landing-place and the schooner from view.

Puggles, who in spite of his shortness of limb had throughout maintained the lead by several rods, suddenly stopped, and fell to shouting and gesticulating wildly. Breaking into a run, Don and Jack speedily came up with him.

"Look, sa'b, look!" gasped Puggles, pointing down the coast with shaking hand.

Far away on the horizon appeared the white canvas of a vessel bowling along before the fresh land breeze, with a fleet of fishing-boats spreading their fustian-hued wings in her wake.

The spot where our adventurers had last seen the schooner at anchor was deserted. She was gone!

CHAPTER IV.

INTRODUCES BOSIN, AND TELLS HOW CAPTAIN MANGO
PROVED HIMSELF A TRUMP.

THE schooner had sailed!
When the dismay caused by this unlooked-for turn of events had somewhat abated, Jack, catching sight of the black boy's lugubrious face, fell to laughing heartily.

"After all," said Don, following his chum's example, "it's no use crying over spilt milk. I'm not sure but this is the best thing that could have happened, Jack."

"My opinion exactly. We began the quest without the guv's knowledge, and *nolens volens* we must continue it without his consent. What's the next piece on the programme, old fellow?"

Don pondered for a moment.

"Why, first," said he, "we must ascertain

whether that fellow told us the truth about the shark-charmer's having gone across the Strait. If it turns out that he has, then I'm not exactly clear yet as to what our next move will be, though I've an idea. You shall hear what it is later on."

"All right," said Jack; "whatever course you decide on, I'm with you heart and fist, anyhow."

Arrived in the vicinity of the bazaar, Puggles was at once despatched to learn what he could of the shark-charmer's movements. In half an hour he returned. His report confirmed that which they had already heard. The shark-charmer had undoubtedly sailed for the opposite side of the Strait.

Throwing himself upon his back in the shade of the banyan tree which had witnessed the discovery of the pearls, Don drew his helmet over his eyes, and pondered long and deeply.

"Jack," said he at length, "how much money have you?"

Jack turned out his pockets.

"Barely a rupee and a half," said he.

"And I," added Don, turning out his own, "have four and a half."

"Here one rupee got, sa'b," cried Puggles, tugging at his waist-cloth. "Me giving him heart and fist, anyhow."

"That makes seven rupees, then," said his master, laughing; "not much to continue the quest on, eh, Jack?"

"We'll manage," said Jack hopefully. "But, I say, you haven't told us your plans yet, old fellow."

"Oh, our course is as plain as a pikestaff. We'll hire a native boat, and follow the shark-charmer across the Strait. The only question is, where's enough money to come from?"

"Don't know," said Jack, "unless we try to borrow it in the bazaar."

At this juncture there occurred an interruption which, unlikely though it may seem, was destined to lead to a most satisfactory solution of this all-important and perplexing question.

While this conversation was in progress Puggles had seated himself at a short distance behind his master, and throwing his turban aside, proceeded to untie and dress the one tuft of hair which adorned the back of his otherwise cleanly shaven head.

Directly above the spot where he sat there

extended far out from the trunk of the banyan a branch of great size, from which dangled numerous rope-like air-roots, which, reaching to within a few feet of the ground, swayed to and fro in the morning breeze. Out along this branch crept a large black monkey, which, after taking a cautious survey of Puggles and his unconscious neighbours, glided noiselessly down one of the swinging roots, and from its extremity dropped lightly to the ground within a yard of the discarded turban. Cautiously, with his cunning ferret-eyes fastened on the preoccupied Puggles, the monkey approached the coveted prize, snatched it up, and with a shrill cry of triumph turned tail and fled.

Looking quickly round at the cry, Puggles took in the situation at a glance.

"Sa'b! Sar!" he shouted, invoking the aid of both his master and Jack in one breath, "one black debil monkey me turban done hooking;" and leaping to his feet he gave chase.

"Why," said Jack, "the little beast is making a bee-line for the old fort. It must be Bosin, Captain Mango's pet monkey."

"Captain Mango!" cried Don, as though seized with some sudden inspiration. "Never thought of him until this minute!" and, clapping on his helmet, he set off at a run after Puggles and the monkey.

Away like the wind went the monkey, the stolen turban trailing after him through the sand like a great serpent; and away went Puggles, his back hair flying. But while Puggles was short of wind, the monkey was nimble of foot. The race was, therefore, unequal from the start, its finish more summary than satisfactory; for as Puggles ran, with his eyes glued upon the scurrying monkey, and his mouth wide-stretched, his foot unluckily came in contact with a tree-root, which lay directly across his path. Immediately beyond was a bed of fine soft sand, and into this he pitched, head foremost. Just then his master came up, with Jack at his heels.

"Sa'b! Sar!" spluttered Puggles, knuckling his eyes and spitting sand right and left, "debil monkey done stole turban. Where him going, sa'b?"

"Come on, Pug," his master called out as he ran past; "your headgear's all right—the monkey's taken it into the fort."

The structure known as "the fort" occupied

the summit of a sandy knoll, about which grew a thick plantation of cocoanut palms, seemingly as ancient as the fort itself. The walls of the enclosure had so crumbled away in places as to afford glimpses of the buildings within. These were two in number—one an ancient *godown*, as dilapidated as the surrounding wall; the other, a bungalow in excellent repair, blazing in all the glory of abundant whitewash.

Towards this building, after passing the tumble-down gateway, with its turreted side-towers alive with pigeons, Don and his companion shaped their course; for this was by no means their first visit to the fort. A broad, low-eaved verandah shaded the front of the bungalow, and upon this opened two or three low windows and a door. As they drew near a shadow suddenly darkened the doorway, and there emerged upon the verandah an individual whose pea-jacket and trousers of generous nautical cut unmistakably proclaimed him to be a seafaring man. About his throat a neckerchief of a deep marine blue was tied in a huge knot; while from beneath the left leg of his wide pantaloons there projected the end of a stout wooden substitute for the real limb.

On catching sight of his visitors an expression of mingled astonishment and pleasure overspread his honest, bronzed features.

"Shiver my binnacle!" roared he, advancing with a series of hitches and extended hand to

THE VISIT TO CAPTAIN MANGO.

meet them. "Shiver my binnacle if it ain't Master Don and Master Jack made port again! An' split my topsails, yonder's the little nigger swab a-bearin' down under full sail out o' the offin'! Lay alongside the old hulk, my hearties, an' tell an old shipmate what may be the meaning of it all. Where away might the schooner be, I axes?"

"To tell you the truth, Captain Mango," said Don, shaking the old sailor by the hand in hearty fashion, "on that point we're as much at sea as yourself. We pulled ashore last night on a little matter of business of our own—without the skipper's knowledge, you understand—and when we returned here this morning the schooner had sailed."

"Shiver my figger-head if ever I hear'd any yarn to beat that!" roared the captain, gripping Jack by the hand in turn. "An' d'ye mean to say now, as ye ain't atween decks, sound asleep in your bunks, when the wessel gets under weigh?"

"Not we," cried Jack, laughing at the captain's puzzled face and earnest manner; "we were miles down the coast just then."

"Belay there!" sang out the captain, rubbing his stubbly chin in greater perplexity than ever. "Blow me if I'm able to make out what tack you're on, lad. For, d'ye see, I lays alongside o' the wessel somewheres about eight bells—arter they fires the signal gun, d'ye see—to pay my 'specks to the master like, and shiver my bulk-head, when I axes what might *your* bearin's be, lads, he ups an' says, 'The younkers be below decks,' says he; an' so he weighs anchor, an' shapes his course for Colombic."

"It's plain there's been a double misunderstanding," said Don; "*we* knew nothing of the guv's intention to sail this morning, and *he* knew nothing of our absence from the schooner. He, of course, thought we were below, and so sailed without us. As I hinted just now, we're ashore on business of our own. Fact is, we're in a fix, and we want your advice."

"Adwice is it?" cried the captain, leading his visitors indoors; "fire away, lads, till I hears what manner o' stuff you wants, and the wery best a water-logged old seaman can give ye, ye shall have—shiver my figger-head if ye shan't! Howsomedever, afore we lays our heads together like, I'll pipe the cook and order ye some wittles."

This hospitable duty performed, the captain threw himself into a chair with his "main-brace," as he jocosely termed his wooden leg, extended before him, and, bidding Don proceed with what he had to say, composed himself to listen. Whereupon Don recounted the cause and manner of the shark-charmer's punishment, the discovery and subsequent loss of the pearls, together with their reasons for suspecting the shark-charmer of the theft, as well as how they had been tricked by the latter's supposed accomplice, and on making their way back to the beach had found, not the schooner as they expected, but a deserted roadstead.

"The thief has crossed the Strait, there's no doubt about that," he concluded. "We want to hire a boat and go in pursuit of him; but the governor's sudden departure has placed us in a dilemma. The fact is, captain, we haven't enough cash to——"

"Belay there!" roared the captain, stumping across the room to a side-table. "Hold hard, lads, till I has a whiff o' the fragrant! Shiver my main-top! there's nothing like tobackie for ilin' up a seaman's runnin' gear, says you!"

Filling a meerschaum pipe of high colour and huge dimensions from a pouch almost as large as a sailor's bag, the captain reseated himself, and for some minutes puffed away in silence.

"Shiver my smokestack!" cried he at last, slapping his thigh energetically with his disengaged hand, "the thing's as easy as boxin' the compass, lads! You axes me for adwice: my adwice is, up anchor and away as soon as ye can. Supplies is low, says you. What o' that? I axes. There's a canvas bag in the old sea-chest yonder as'll charter all the boats hereabouts, if so be as they're wanted, which they ain't, d'ye mind me. Ye can dror on the canvas bag, lads, an' welcome —why not? I axes. An' there's as tight a leetle cutter in the boat-house below as ever ye clapped eyes on—which the *Jolly Tar*'s her name—what's at your sarvice, shiver my main-brace if it ain't! An' blow me, as the fog-horn says to the donkey-engine, I'll ship along with ye, lads!

> "An' a-sailin' we'll go, we'll go;
> An' a-sailin' we will go-o-o!"

he concluded, with a stave of a rollicking old sea-song.

"Hurrah! You're a trump, captain, and no mistake!" cried Jack, while Don sprang forward and gripped the old sailor's hand with a heartiness that showed how thoroughly he appreciated this generous offer.

"Why, y'see, lads," explained the captain apologetically, "'twould be ekal to a-sendin' of ye to Davy Jones if I was to let ye go pokin' round this 'ere Strait alone. Now me—rope-yarn an' marlin-spikes!—there ain't a reef, nor a shool, nor yet a crik atween Colombie an' Jafna P'int but what's laid down on this 'ere old chart o' mine," tapping his forehead significantly. "An' besides,

I'm a-spilin' for a bit o' the briny, so with you I ships—an' why not? I axes."

"And right glad of your company and assistance we'll be, captain," said Don. "The main difficulty will be, of course, to discover to what part of the Indian coast the thief has gone."

The captain puffed thoughtfully at his pipe.

"Why, as for that," said he at length, "I've an idee as I knows his reckonin', shiver my binnacle if I ain't! But that's neither here nor there at this present speakin'. Ballast's the first consideration, lads; so dror up your cheers an' tackle the perwisions."

When they had complied with this welcome invitation to the entire satisfaction of the captain and their own appetites, "Now, lads," said the old sailor gaily, "do ye turn in an' snatch a wink o' sleep, whiles I goes an' gets the cutter ready for puttin' to sea. For, says you, look alive's the word if so be as we wants to overhaul the warmint as took the treasure in tow. Spike my guns!—we'll make him heave to in no time!

> "For all things is ready, an' nothing we want,
>   To fit out our ship as rides so close by;
> Both wittles an' weapons, they be nothing scant,
>   Like worthy sea-dogs ourselves we will try!"

Trolling this ditty, the captain stumped away, while his guests made themselves as comfortable as they could, and sought the slumber of which they stood so much in need.

It was late in the afternoon when they woke. Puggles had disappeared. Proceeding to the beach, they found the captain, assisted by a small army of native servants, busily engaged in putting the finishing touches to his preparations for the proposed voyage. Just above the surf-line lay the *Jolly Tar*—a trim little craft, fitted with mast and sprit, whose sharp, clean-cut lines betokened possibilities in the way of speed that promised well for the issue of their enterprise. In the cuddy, amid a bewildering array of pots, pans, and pannikins, Puggles had already installed himself, his shining face a perfect picture of self-complacent good-nature, whilst Bosin, newly released from durance vile, sat in the stern-sheets, cracking nuts and jabbering defiance at his black rival.

"A purty craft!" chuckled the captain, checking for a moment the song that was always on his lips, as he led his visitors to the cutter's side; "stave my water-butt if there's anything can pull ahead of her in these 'ere parts. Everything ship-shape an' ready to hand, d'ye see—wittles for the woyage, an' drink for the woyagers. Likewise ammunitions o' war," cried he proudly, pointing out a number of muskets and shining cutlasses, which a servant just then brought up and placed on board.

> "Both wittles an' weapons, they be nothing scant,
> So like worthy sea-dogs ourselves we will try."

"What with the cutlasses and guns, and the captain's wooden leg, to say nothing of our small-arms, Don," said Jack, "we'd better set up for buccaneers at once."

"Shiver my main-brace! a wooden leg ain't sich a bad article arter all," rejoined the captain; "specially when a seaman falls overboard. With a life-buoy o' that nater rove on to his starn-sheets, he's sartin to keep one leg above water, says you."

"No doubt of that, even if he goes down by the head," assented Don, laughing. "But, I say, captain, what's in the keg—spirits?"

"Avast there!" replied the captain, half shutting one eye and contemplating the keg with the other, "that 'ere keg, lads, has stuff in its hold what's a sight better'n spurts. Gunpowder, lads, that's what it is; and spike my guns if we don't broach the same to the health of old Salambo when we falls in with him. What say you, lads?

"We always be ready,
Steady, lads, steady;
We'll fight an' we'll conquer agin an' agin."

"I hope we shan't have to do that, captain," said Jack gravely. "But powder or no powder, we'll pay the beggar out, anyhow."

"Right, lad; so we'll just take the keg along with us in case of emargencies like. Shiver my compass, there's no telling aforehand what this 'ere wenture may lead to."

To whatever the venture was destined to lead, preparations for its successful inception went on apace, and by nightfall all was in readiness. The captain declaring that he "couldn't abide the ways o' them 'ere jabbering nigger swabs when afloat,' the only addition to their numbers was a single trusty servant of the old sailor's, who was taken along rather with a view to the cutter's safety when they should be ashore than because his assistance was required in sailing her.

Don having despatched an overland messenger with a letter to his father, explaining their absence and proposed undertaking, as the full moon rose out of the eastern sea the cutter was launched.

Half an hour later, with her white sails bellying before the freshening land-breeze, she bore away for the opposite shore of the Strait, on that quest from which one at least of those on board was destined never to return.

While her sails were yet visible in the moonlit offing, a native crept down to the deserted beach. He was a dark-skinned, evil-featured fellow; and the moonlight, falling upon his face, showed his left temple to be swollen and discoloured as from a recent blow. On his shoulder he carried a paddle and a boathook.

"The wind will drop just before dawn," he muttered, as he stood a moment noting the strength and direction of the breeze. "Then, you white devil, then!" and he patted the boathook affectionately, as if between him and it there existed some secret, dark understanding.

Selecting a *ballam* or "dug-out" from amongst a number that lay there, he placed the boathook carefully in the bottom of the frail skiff, and launched it almost in the furrow which the cutter's keel had ploughed in the yielding sand. Then springing in, and plying his paddle with rapid strokes, he quickly disappeared in the cutter's wake.

THE LASCAR LAUNCHES THE BALLAM.

[*Page* 52.

CHAPTER V.

THE LASCAR GETS HIS KNIFE BACK.

HER light sails winged to catch every breath of the light but steady breeze that chased her astern, the cutter for some hours bowled through the water merrily. In the cabin Puggles and the captain's black servant snored side by side; whilst Don and Jack lolled comfortably just abaft the mast, where the night wind, soft and spicy as the breath of Eden, would speedily have lulled them to slumber but for the excitement that fired their blood. The captain was at the tiller, Bosin curled up by his side.

"If this 'ere wind holds, lads," exclaimed the old sailor abruptly, after a prolonged silence on his part, "we'd orter make the island agin sunrise, shiver my forefoot if we don't!"

Don looked up with half-sleepy interest. "Island, captain? I thought we were heading straight for the Indian coast."

"Ay, so we be, straight away. But, y'see, lad, as I hinted a while back, I has a sort o' innard idee, so to say, as the old woman ain't on the mainland.'

"What old woman?" queried Jack, yawning. "Didn't know there was one in the case, captain."

The old sailor burst into a roar of laughter. "An' no more there ain't, lad," chuckled he; "an' slit my hammock if we wants one, says you. Forty odd year has I sailed the seas, an' hain't signed articles with any on 'em yet. A tight leetle wessel's the lass for me, lads; for, unship my helm! *she* never takes her own head for it, says you."

"Then what about the old woman you mentioned, captain?" said Don banteringly.

"Avast there now! An' d'ye mean to say," demanded the captain incredulously, "as you ain't ever hear'd tell o' the fish what sails under that 'ere name? And a wicious warmint he is, too, shiver my keelson! Hysters is his wittles, an' pearls his physic; he lives on 'em, so to say; an' so I calls the cove as took them pearls o' your'n in tow an old woman; an' why not, I axes?"

"But what about the island you spoke of just now, captain?"

"Why, d'ye see, it's this way, lads; there's an island off the coast ahead, a sort o' holy place like, where them thievin' natives goes once a year an' gets salwation from their sins. Howsomedever, that's neither here nor there, says you; the p'int's this, lads: Somewheres about the month o' March, which is this same month, says you, here the priests flocks from all parts, an' here they stays until they gets a purty pocketful o' cash. Now, my idee's this, d'ye see: the old woman—which I means Salambo—lays alongside the schooner an' takes them pearls o' your'n in tow. What for? says you. Cash, says I. An' so, shiver my mainbrace, he shapes his course for this 'ere island, an' sells 'em to the priests."

"Very likely," assented Don. "He's bound to carry them to the best market, of course."

"And equally of course the best market is where the most priests are. By Jove, you *have* a headpiece, captain!" put in Jack.

"I'm afraid, though," resumed Don, after a moment's silence, "I'm afraid it's not going to be so easy to come at the old fellow as we think. You say this island's a sort of holy place; well, it's bound to be packed with natives to the very surf-line in that case. Rather ticklish work, I should think, taking the old fellow among so many pals. There's the getting ashore, too; what's to prevent their sighting us?"

"Belay there!" roared the captain, vigorously thumping the bottom of the boat with his wooden leg. "Shiver my main-brace! what sort o' craft do ye take me for, I axes? A island's a island the world over—a lump o' land what's floated out to sea. Wery good, that bein' so—painters an' boathooks!—ain't it as easy a-boardin' of her through the starn-ports as along o' the fore-chains?"

"Oh, you mean to make the back of the island, and steal a march on old Salambo from the rear, then?" cried Don. "A capital idea!"

"You're on the right tack there, lad," assented the captain. "There's as purty a leetle cove at the backside o' that island as ever wessel cast anchor in, an' well I knows it, shiver my binnacle! Daylight orter put us into it, if so be—— Split my sprit-sail, lads, if it ain't a-fallin' calm!"

An ominous flapping of the cutter's sails confirmed the captain's words. During the half-hour over which this conversation extended the wind

BECALMED IN THE MOONLIGHT.

[*Page* 57.

had gradually died away until scarcely a movement of the warm night air could be felt. The cutter, losing her headway, rolled lazily to the motion of the long, glassy swell. Consulting his watch, Don announced it to be three o'clock.

"This 'ere's the lull atween the sea-breeze an' the land-breeze," observed the captain complacently, working the tiller from side to side as if trying to coax renewed life into the cutter. "Howsomedever, it hadn't orter last long. Stow my sea-chest!—we'll turn in an' catch a wink o' sleep atween whiles. Here, Master Jack, lad! take a turn at the tiller, will 'ee?"

Settling himself in the captain's place, with instructions to call that worthy sea-dog should the wind freshen, Jack began his first watch. Becalmed as they were, the tiller was useless, so he let it swing, contenting himself with keeping a bright look-out. But soon he concluded even this to be an unnecessary precaution. Not a sail was to be seen on the moonlit expanse of ocean; and even had a score been in sight, there would still have been no danger whatever, in the absence of wind, of their interfering with the cutter. In fine, so secure did he consider their position, and so soporific an influence did the comfortable snoring of Don and the captain exercise upon him, that in a very short time his head sank upon his breast, and he fell asleep.

He had slept soundly for perhaps an hour, when a cold touch upon the cheek startled him into consciousness.

Rousing himself, he found Bosin at his elbow. The monkey for some reason had left his master's side, and it was his clammy paw, Jack now perceived, that had awakened him. It almost looked as if the monkey had purposely interrupted his slumber. But what had roused the monkey? Jack rose to his feet, stretched himself, and looked about him.

The night was, if anything, more breathlessly calm than when he had relieved the captain. Upon the unruffled, deserted sea the moonlight shimmered with a brilliancy uncanny in its ghostliness. From the cutter straight away to and around the horizon not an object, so far as he could make out, darkened the surface of the water, except under the cutter's larboard bow, where the moon-cast shadow of the sail fell. He fancied he saw something move there, close under the bow where the shadow lay blackest. The next instant it had disappeared.

to his assistance. Before either well knew what had actually happened, Jack was alongside.

"What's the matter? Are you hurt?" Don inquired anxiously, giving him a hand over the side.

"Hurt? No, not a scratch," said Jack lightly, scrambling inboard, and proceeding to wring the water from his dripping garments. "A narrow squeak, though. That lascar villain has got his knife back, anyhow."

"Who?" cried Don in amazement; for, amid the confusion, neither he nor the captain had seen the native.

"The lascar. What else do you suppose I went over the side for? I dozed off, you see, captain," said Jack, as the old sailor came stumping up with extended hand, "and that lascar dog, who must have seen us sail and paddled after us, stole a march on me, and tried to crack my nut with a boathook. Lucky for me, he ran his canoe against the side and woke me up. Got on my feet just in time to dodge the blow. Then he smashed the boathook through the side. By Jove! I forgot that. We must stop the leak, or we'll fill in no time."

"Stave my quarter!" roared the captain, detaining him as he was about to rush aft. "The leak's stopped, lad; but blow me if ever I hear'd anything to beat this 'ere yarn o' your'n, so spin us the rest on it."

"That's soon done," resumed Jack. "When I found the fellow wouldn't give me a fair show, I boarded him, captain, and treated him to a few inches of cold steel. He won't trouble us again, I reckon!"

Scarcely had he finished speaking when Don gripped his arm and pointed to where, a dozen yards away, the bottom of the canoe glistened in the moonlight. A dark object had suddenly appeared alongside the overturned skiff. Presently a surging splash was heard.

"Shiver my keelson if he ain't righted the craft!" roared the captain, snatching up one of the muskets as the lascar was seen to scramble into the canoe and paddle slowly away.

Don laid a quick hand upon the old sailor's arm.

"Let the beggar go," said he. "He'll never reach land with that knife in him."

"Maybe not, lad," replied the captain, shaking off the hold upon his arm and taking

"All right, Bosin, old chap," said he, stroking the monkey's back; "a false alarm this time—back to your quarters, old fellow!"

The monkey, as if reassured by these words, crept away to his master's side, whilst Jack resumed his seat, and again dozed off.

Not for long, however. It was not the monkey this time, but a sudden and by no means gentle thud against the cutter's side that roused him. Awake in an instant, he sprang to his feet with a startled exclamation. Close under the cutter's quarter lay a canoe, and in the canoe there stood erect a native, with what appeared to be a boat-hook poised above his head. All this Jack took in at a glance.

"Boat ahoy! Who's that?" he cried sharply, his hand instinctively seeking the knife at his belt.

For answer came a savage, muttered imprecation; and the boathook, impelled with all the strength of the native's muscular arms, descended swiftly through the air. Starting aside, Jack received the blow upon his left arm, off which the heavy, iron-shod weapon glanced, striking the gun'le of the boat with a resounding crash.

"The lascar!" muttered Jack between his

teeth, as he stepped back a pace and whipped out his knife in anticipation of a renewal of the attack.

But the lascar, baffled in his attempt to take his enemy by surprise, did not repeat the blow. Instead, he drew off, and with all his strength drove the iron point of the boathook through the cutter's side below the water-line.

"By Heaven!" cried Jack, as he perceived his intention, "I'll soon settle scores with you, my fine fellow."

Springing lightly upon the gun'le, at a single bound he cleared the few yards of open water intervening between the cutter and the canoe, and with all the impetus of his leap drove the knife into the lascar's shoulder up to the very hilt.

The lascar went overboard like a log. The canoe overturning at the same instant, Jack followed him.

The noise of the scuffle having roused the sleepers, all was now wild commotion on board the cutter; Captain Mango roaring out his strange nautical oaths, and stumping hither and thither in search of something with which to stop the leak; Don shouting wildly at Jack, as he hastily threw off shoes and coat to swim the best aim he could, considering the motion of the boat. "Bloodshed's best awoided, says you. Wery good; an' the best way to awoid it, d'ye mind me, is to send yon warmint to Davy Jones straight away. Consequential, the quality o' marcy shan't be strained on this 'ere occasion, as the whale says when he swallied the school o' codlings." And with that he fired.

The lascar was seen to discontinue the use of his paddle for a moment, and then to make off faster than before.

The old sailor's face fell.

"Spike my guns, I've gone and missed the warmint!" said he. "Howsomedever, we'll meet again, as the shark's lower jaw says to the upper 'un when they parted company to accomidate the sailor. An' blow me, lads, here comes the wind!

"Ay, here's a master excelleth in skill,
   An' the master's mate he is not to seek;
An' here's a Bosin ull do our good will,
   An' a ship, d'ye see, lads, as never had leak.
So lustily, lustily, let us sail forth!
Our sails be right trim an' the wind's to the north!"

It was now five o'clock, and as day broke the cutter, with a freshening breeze on her starboard quarter, bore away for the island, now in full view. When about a mile short of it, however, the captain laid the boat's head several points nearer the wind, and shaped his course as though running past it for the mainland, which lay like a low bank of mist on the horizon. In the cuddy Puggles was busy with preparations for breakfast, whilst Don lolled on the rail, watching the shore, and idly trailing one hand in the water.

"Hullo! what's this?" he exclaimed suddenly, examining with interest a fragment of dripping cloth that had caught on his hand. "Jack, come here!"

Jack happened to be forward just then, hanging out his drenched clothes to dry upon an improvised line, but hearing Don's exclamation, he sprang aft. Somehow he was always expecting surprises now.

"Look here," said Don, rapidly spreading out the soaked cloth upon his knee, "have you ever seen this before?"

"Not likely!—a mere scrap of rag that some greasy native——" Jack began, eyeing the said scrap of rag contemptuously. But suddenly his tone changed, and he gasped out: "By Jove, old fellow, it's not the handkerchief, is it?"

"The very same!" replied Don, rising and hurrying aft to where the captain stood at the tiller. "I say, captain, you remember my telling you how I tied a handkerchief round that bag of pearls? Well, here's the identical 'wipe,' with my initials on it as large as life. Just fished it out of the water."

For full a minute the old sailor stared at him open-mouthed. Then:

"Flush my scuppers," roared he, "if this 'ere ain't the tidiest piece o' luck as ever I run agin. We've got the warmint safe in the maintop, so to say, where he can't run away—shiver my mainbrace if we ain't!"

"Thanks to your clear head, captain," said Don. "It certainly does look as if he had come straight to the island here."

"We'll purty soon know for sartin; we're a-makin' port hand over fist," rejoined the captain, bringing the cutter's head round, and running under the lee of the island.

This side, unlike the wind-swept seaward face, was thickly clad in jungle, above which at intervals towered a solitary palm like a sentinel on duty. No traces of human habitation were to be seen; for a rocky backbone or ridge, running lengthwise

F

of the island, isolated its frequented portion from this jungly half. Midway between the extremities of this ridge rose two hills: one a symmetrical, cone-shaped elevation, clad in a mantle of jungle green; the other a vast mass of naked rock, towering hundreds of feet in air, and in its general outline somewhat resembling a colossal kneeling elephant. As if to heighten the resemblance, there was perched upon the lofty back a native temple, which looked for all the world like a gigantic howdah.

"D'ye see them elewations, lads?" cried the captain, heading the cutter straight for what appeared to be an unbroken line of jungle. "A brace o' twins, says you. Wery good; atween 'em lies as purty a leetle cove as wessel ever cast anchor in—slip my cable if it ain't!"

"Are you sure you're not out of your reckoning, captain?" said Jack, scanning the shore-line with dubious eye. "It's no thoroughfare, so far as I can see."

"Avast there! What d'ye say to that, now?" chuckled the captain, as the cutter, in obedience to a movement of the tiller, swept round a tiny eyot indistinguishable in its mantle of green from the shore itself, and entered a narrow, land-locked creek, whose precipitous sides were completely covered from summit to water-line with a rank growth of vegetation. "Out with the oars, lads! a steam-whistle couldn't coax a wind into the likes o' this place, says you."

The oars run out, they pulled for some distance through this remarkable rift in the hills, the cutter's mast in places sweeping the overhanging jungle; until at last a spot was reached where a side ravine cleft the cliff upon their left, terminating at the water's edge in a strip of sandy beach, thickly shaded with cocoa-nut palms.

"Stow my cargo!" chuckled the captain, as he ran the cutter bow-on into the sand, "a nautical sea-sarpent himself couldn't smell us out here, says you. So here we heaves to, and here we lies until——swabs an' slush-buckets, what's this?"

For the captain had already scrambled ashore, and as he uttered these words he stooped and intently examined the sand at his feet. In it were visible recent footprints, and a long trailing furrow that started from the water's edge and ran for several yards straight up the beach. Where the furrow terminated there lay a native *ballam*.

Jack was first to espy the canoe. Guessing the cause of the captain's sudden excitement, he ran up the sands to the spot where the rude vessel lay. The *ballam* was still dripping sea-water; and in it, amid a pool of blood, lay a sailor's sheath-knife.

"The lascar!" he shouted, snatching up the blood-stained weapon, and holding it out at arm's length, as Don and the captain hurried up; "we've landed in his very tracks!"

CHAPTER VI.

IN THE THICK OF IT.

EITHER the lascar's wound had not proved as serious as Jack surmised, or the fellow was endowed with as many lives as a cat. At all events, he had reached land before them, and in safety.

"Sharks an' sea-sarpents!" fumed the captain, stumping excitedly round and round the canoe. "The warmint had orter been sent to Davy Jones as I adwised. Howsomedever, bloodshed's best awoided, says you, Master Don, lad; an' so, shiver my keelson! here we lies stranded. What's the course to be steered now, I axes? That's a matter o' argyment, says you; so here's for a whiff o' the fragrant!"

Bidding his servant fetch pipe and tobacco, the captain seated himself upon the canoe and fell to puffing meditatively, his companions meanwhile discussing the situation and a project of their own, with many anxious glances in the direction of the adjacent jungle, where, for anything they knew to the contrary, the lascar might even then be stealthily watching their movements.

"Shiver my smokestack! d'ye see that, now?" exclaimed the captain at last, following with half-closed eye and tarry finger the ascent of a perfect smoke-ring that had just left his lips. "An' what's a ring o' tobackie smoke? says you. A forep'intin' to ewents to come, says I. A ring means surrounded, d'ye see; an'—grape-shot an' gun-swabs!—surrounded means fightin', lads!"

"Fun or fighting, I'm ready, anyhow!" cried Jack, flourishing his knife.

"Ay, ay, lad; an' me, too, for the matter o' that," replied the old sailor, presenting his pipe at an imaginary foe like a pistol; "but when our sitiwation an' forces is beknownst to the enemy, we're sartin to be surprised, d'ye mind me. An' so I gets an idee!

"Go patter to lubbers an' swabs, d'ye see,
'Bout danger, an' fear, an' the like;
A tight leetle boat an' good sea-room give me,
An' it ain't to a leetle I'll strike!"

"Out with the idea then, captain!" cried Don.

"Shiver my cutlass, lads!—we must carry the

war into the camp o' the enemy, d'ye see. Wery good, that bein' so, what we wants, d'ye mind me, is a safe, tidy place to fall back on, as can't be took, or looted, or burnt, like the cutter here, whiles we're away on the rampage, so to say."

"Why not entrench ourselves on the hill just above?" suggested Jack.

"Stow my sea-chest!—the wery identical plan I perposes," promptly replied the captain. "An' why? you naterally axes. Because it's ha'nted, says I."

"Because it's what?" cried the two young men in chorus. "Haunted?"

"Ay, the abode o' spurts," continued the captain. "There's a old ancient temple aloft on yon hill, d'ye see, as they calls the 'Ha'nted Pagodas'—which they say as it's a tiger-witch or summat inhabits it, d'ye see—an' shiver my binnacle if a native'll go a-nigh it day or night!"

"Admirable! But what about the cutter, captain?" said Don.

The captain sucked for a moment at his pipe as if seeking to draw a suitable idea therefrom.

"What o' the cutter? you axes," said he presently. "Why, we'll warp her down the crik a bit, d'ye see, an' stow her away out o' sight where the wegitation's thickish-like on the face o' the cliff; copper my bottom if we won't!"

"The stores, of course, must be carried up the hill," said Jack, entering readily into the captain's plans. "We should set about the job at once."

"Avast there, lad! What's to perwent the jungle hereabouts a-usin' of its eyes? I axes. The wail o' night, says you. So, when the wail o' night unfurls, as the poic says, why, up the hill they goes."

This being unanimously agreed to, and Puggles at that moment announcing breakfast, our trio of adventurers adjourned to the cutter.

"Captain," said Don, after delighting the black boy's heart by a ravenous attack upon the eatables, "like you, I've got an idee—Hullo, you, Pug! What are you grinning at?"

"Nutting, sa'b," replied Puggles, clapping his hand over his mouth; "only when marster plenty eating, he sometimes bery often one idee getting. Plenty food go inside, he kicking idee out!"

"Just double reef those lips of yours, Pug, and tell us where do *your* ideas come from?" said Jack, laughing.

"Me tinking him here got, sar," said Puggles, gravely patting his waistband, at which the old sailor nearly choked.

"And a pretty stock of them you have, too, judging by the size of your apple-cart!" said his master, shying a biscuit at his head. "Well, as I was saying, captain, I have an idea——"

"Flush my scuppers!" gasped the old sailor, swallowing a brimming pannikin of coffee to clear his throat. "Let's hear more on it then, lad."

"Well, it's this. Jack and I are going over to the town—where the temples are, you understand—to see if we can't sight old Salambo. A bit of reconnoitring may be of use to us later, you see."

"A-goin'—over—to—the—town!" roared the captain in amazement, separating the words as though each were a reluctant step in the direction proposed. "Scuttle my cutter, lads! ye'll have the whole pack o' warmints down on ye in a brace o' shakes!"

"You won't say so when you see us in full war-paint," retorted Jack, as he and Don rose and disappeared in the cuddy.

In the course of half an hour the cuddy door was thrown open, and two stalwart young natives, in full country dress, confronted the old sailor. With the assistance of Puggles and the captain's "boy," not to mention soot from the cuddy pots, the two young fellows had cleverly "made up" in the guise of Indian pilgrims. At first sight of them the captain, thinking old Salambo's crew were upon him, seized a musket and threw himself into an attitude of defence.

"Blow me!" he roared, when a loud burst of laughter apprised him of his mistake, "if this ain't the purtiest go as ever I see. Scrapers an' holystones, ye might lay alongside the old woman himself, lads, an' him not know ye from a reglar, genewine brace o' lying niggers. What tack are ye on now, lads? I axes."

"Off to the town, captain," replied Don, "to search for old Salambo among his idols. That is, if you'll let Spottie here come with us as pilot."

"Spottie" was the nickname with which they had dubbed the captain's black servant, whose face was deeply pitted from smallpox.

"Right, lads; he's been here afore, an' knows the lay o' the land; so take him in tow, and welcome," was the captain's hearty rejoinder. "An' stow your knives away amidships, in case of emargency like ; though blow me if they ever take ye for aught but genewine lying niggers!"

Concealing their knives about their persons in accordance with this advice, they launched the lascar's *ballam* upon the creek—which the captain assured them expanded a little further inland into a broad lagoon, too deep to ford—and so set out. The paddle had been removed; but as the creek appeared to have nowhere, in its upper reaches at any rate, a greater depth than half-a-dozen feet, the boathook served admirably as a substitute for propelling the canoe.

"What's the line for, Spottie?" Jack asked, seeing their guide throw a coil of small rope into the canoe, which he afterwards boarded in person and shoved off.

"Turkle, sar," replied Spottie. "Plenty time me catching big turkle asleep on sand. He no come in *ballam*, so me taking rope to tow him astern. Him bery nice soup making, sar," said Spottie, who had always an eye to anything potable.

Little as they guessed it then, this line was to play a more unique and serviceable part in the day's adventures than that indicated by the souploving Spottie.

The creek, as the captain had intimated, presently expanded into a lagoon fully a quarter of a mile wide, and so shallow in parts that the canoe almost touched the amber-coloured sands over which it passed. Arrived at the further side, they drew the canoe upon the beach, and continued their route to the town by way of a steep jungle-path, which, in the course of some fifteen minutes' hard climbing, led them to the crest of the rocky ridge. Here they paused a moment to look about them.

To the left lay Haunted Pagoda Hill; on their right the colossal Elephant Rock; and, nestling at its base, the native town, with its sea of dun roofs and gleaming white temples. The stirring ramp of tom-toms, and the hoarse roar of the multitude, floated up to them as they stood contemplating the scene.

"Now for it!" cried Jack, heading the descent. "We'll soon be in the thick of it, anyhow."

A few minutes more and they stood on the outskirts of the town.

"Make for the chief temple, Spottie," said Don to their guide; "and whatever you do, don't call us sahib or sir. We're only pilgrims like yourself, you understand. And say, Spottie, do you know old Salambo, the shark-charmer, when you see him?"

By a nod Spottie intimated that he did.

"Good! He's the chap we're after, you understand. Keep a sharp look-out, and if you happen to get your eye on him——"

"Or on a lascar with a knife-wound in his shoulder," put in Jack.

"Just pull my cloth, will you?" concluded Don.

Again the trusty Spottie nodded, and at a signal led the way into the main-street, where they immediately found themselves in the midst of a noisy, surging crowd of natives.

So perfect was their disguise, however, that Don could not detect a single suspicious glance directed towards them.

The natives who thronged the street were, to a man, heading for the temples. Into these, if nothing was seen of the shark-charmer outside, Don was resolved to penetrate.

As no English foot is ever allowed—in Southern India, at least—to cross the threshold of a Hindu shrine, this was a step attended with tremendous risk. Detection would mean fighting for their lives against overwhelming odds.

"We'll do it, however," said Don resolutely. "The temple's the place to look for him, since he's a priest, and in this disguise the pearls are worth the risk."

That this was also Jack's opinion was plain from the resolute, nonchalant manner in which he pressed forward.

Owing to the congested state of the thoroughfare, progress was necessarily slow. They were more than an hour in gaining the open *maidan* in which the street terminated.

In the centre of this open space lay a sacred tank, flanked, on that side nearest the Elephant Rock, by a vast semicircle of temples. Midway in this line stood the chief temple. Here, if at all, the shark-charmer would most likely be found.

But to reach the chief temple was no easy task. Vast crowds of pilgrims surrounded the sacred tank, awaiting their turn to bathe in its stagnant green waters.

At last, after much elbowing and pushing, they reached the steps of the chief temple. Thus far they had seen nothing of Salambo. As they had already made the entire circuit of the tank, there was nothing for it but to seek him in the sacred edifice itself.

Spottie led the way, since for him there was absolutely no risk. Following close upon his heels, past the hideous stone monsters which flanked the entrance, the mock pilgrims found themselves in the temple court. Here the crush was even greater than without.

They had now reached the crucial point of their adventure.

A single unguarded word or action on their part, and each man of these teeming thousands would instantly become a mortal enemy!

Don strove to appear unconcerned, but his pulses throbbed madly at the mere thought of detection. As for Jack, the careless poise of his right hand at his belt showed him to be on his guard, though he looked as cool as a sea-breeze.

Over the heads of the multitude, on the opposite side of the court, could be seen an inner shrine, where offerings were being made. Selecting this as his goal, Don began to edge his way slowly but steadily towards it, closely followed by Spottie and the undaunted Jack.

Suddenly he felt a· hand tugging at his cloth. Unable to turn himself about in the crush, he twisted his head round and caught Spottie's eye. By a quick, almost imperceptible movement of hand and head, the black directed his attention towards the left. Looking in the direction thus indicated, Don saw, but a few yards away, the portly person of the shark-charmer.

By dint of persistent pushing, he presently succeeded in approaching so near to his man that, had he so wished, he could have laid a hand upon his shoulder.

The shark-charmer was evidently bent upon gaining the inner shrine at the opposite side of the court. Inch by inch he pummelled his way through the dense crowd, unconscious that the sahibs whom he had robbed were dogging his steps. Once when he turned his head his eyes actually rested upon Don's face. But he failed to recognise him, and so went on again, greatly to Don's relief.

Then of a sudden the limit of the crush was reached, and they emerged upon a comparatively clear space immediately in front of the shrine. This the shark-charmer crossed without hesitation, but Don hung back, uncertain whether it would be prudent to venture further. However, seeing a group of natives about to approach the shrine with offerings, he joined them, and in company with Jack ascended the steps.

The shark-charmer had already disappeared within.

Fumbling in his cloth for some small coin to present as an offering, Don crossed the threshold, and was in the very act of penetrating the dimly-

IN THE TEMPLE.

lighted, incense-clouded chamber just beyond, when a guarded exclamation from Jack caused him to glance quickly over his shoulder.

Following them with the stealthy tread of a panther was a swarthy, evil-looking native.

"The lascar!" said Jack, in a low, breathless

whisper. "Back, old fellow, for your life! Once in the crowd, we're safe."

Back they darted towards the entrance, but the lascar, anticipating this manœuvre, was on his guard. As Jack dashed past, the cunning spy thrust out his foot and sent him sprawling on the flagstones. Don, hearing the noise, turned back to his friend's assistance, and by the time Jack regained his feet the lascar had reached the entrance and raised the hue-and-cry.

"This way!" cried Don, making for a narrow side door, as the lascar's shouts began to echo through the precincts of the temple. "Get your knife ready, he's raised the alarm!"

Through the door they dashed, only to find themselves in the court, hemmed in on every side. The frenzied cries of the lascar continued to ring through the enclosure; but, fortunately for the mock pilgrims, so vast was the concourse of natives, and so deafening the uproar, that only those nearest the shrine understood his words, while even they failed as yet to penetrate the clever disguise of the intruders. This gave them time to draw breath and look about them.

Close on their left Jack's quick eye discovered an exit, about which the crowd was less dense than elsewhere. The great doors stood wide open, disclosing a narrow street. Between this exit and the spot where they stood at bay, a number of sacred bulls were quietly feeding off a great heap of corn which the devotees had poured out upon the flags of the court. All this Jack's eyes took in at a glance.

A roar, terrific as that of ten thousand beasts of prey, burst from the surging multitude. The lascar's words were understood. Glancing quickly over his shoulder, Jack saw that this man, from his place upon the steps of the shrine, was pointing them out.

Another instant, and their disguise would avail them nothing; the maddened, fanatical crowd would be upon them.

"Don," he said, in rapid, husky tones, as he grasped his friend's hand for what he believed to be the last time, "there's but one chance left us, and that's a slim one. You see the door on our left, and those bulls? Do you take one of the two big fellows feeding side by side, and I'll take the other. Use your knife to guide the brute, and with God's help——"

A tremendous roar of voices and a thunderous rush of feet cut his words short.

"Now for it, old fellow!"

With one swift backward glance at the furious human wave sweeping down upon them, they darted towards the bulls, of which the two largest, accustomed to the daily tumult of town and temple, were still composedly feeding, their muzzles buried deep in the mound of corn.

Before the animals had time to lift their heads, the mock pilgrims were on their backs and plying knives and heels upon their sleek flanks.

Bellowing with pain and terror, the bulls, with tails erect and heads lowered, charged the throng about the doorway, bowling them over in all directions like so many ninepins. Before the infuriated crowd in their rear understood the meaning of this unexpected manoeuvre, the mock pilgrims were in the street.

It was a side street, fortunately, separated from the densely-packed *maidan* by a high brick wall, and but few natives were about. Those who followed them out of the temple, too, they soon distanced, for their ungainly steeds made capital time.

But now a new, if less serious, danger menaced them. Apart from the difficulty of clinging to the round, arched backs of the bulls, once started, the maddened animals could not be stopped. Fortunately, they took the direction of the hill-path.

On they tore, bellowing madly, and scattering showers of foam and sand right and left, until, in an amazingly brief space of time, they reached the outskirts of the town. Here, as if divining that their services were no longer required, the bulls stopped abruptly, shooting their riders off their backs into the sand with scant ceremony.

"Regular buck-jumpers!" groaned Jack, rubbing his lacerated shins ruefully. "Glad we're safe out of it, anyhow."

"So am I. But I wonder where Spottie is?" said Don, fanning himself with the loosened end of his turban.

Jack started up. "Never once thought of Spottie since we entered the shrine," cried he. "Come, we must go back and look him up."

Their uneasiness on Spottie's account, however, was at that instant set at rest by the precipitate appearance on the scene of Spottie himself. Seeing his masters charge the crowd on the bulls' backs, he had extricated himself from the crush, and followed them with all possible speed.

"Dey coming, sar!" he panted, as he ran

up. "Lascar debil done fetching plenty black man!"

And there swelled up from the street below a tumult of voices that left no doubt as to the accuracy of his statement.

CHAPTER VII.

"FUN OR FIGHTING, I'M READY, ANYHOW!"

"DEY coming, sar!" groaned Spottie; and even as he spoke the leaders of the mob came tearing round the corner.

"Is it fight or run, Don?" said Jack quietly, adjusting his turban with one hand and laying the other significantly upon his knife.

"No two ways about that! We could never stand against such odds; so we'll run first and fight afterwards."

"And reverse the old saying, eh?" laughed Jack. "I should dearly love to have a whack at them; but if you say run, why—run it is, so here goes!"

Shaking his fist at the howling mob, he sprang up the steep hill-path, followed closely by Don. Spottie had already made good use of his legs, but they soon caught him up, whereupon Jack seized the terrified native by the arm and dragged him over the brow of the ridge.

Down the further side they dashed, breathing easier now, for their movements were here well concealed by the dense jungle through which the pathway ran. As they emerged panting upon the sandy shore of the lagoon, a yell from the hill behind told them that their pursuers had gained the crest of the ridge. At the same instant Don pulled up abruptly, and being too much out of breath to speak, pointed in the direction of the canoe. Beside it stood a couple of natives, who, on seeing them, turned and fled towards the jungle.

"The tall fellow!" shouted Jack. "Stop him! He's got the boathook!"

The boathook was their only means of propelling the canoe. That gone, they were practically at the mercy of their enemies.

After the flying natives they dashed, Jack leading. He quickly came up with the hindermost, whom he dealt a blow that stretched him senseless in the sand. But the fellow who carried the boathook was long of leg and fresh of wind; while Jack was still a dozen yards in his rear, he gained the jungle and disappeared.

"No good!" groaned Jack, as he relinquished the pursuit and turned back. "There's nothing for it but to fight. I say, Don, what's up?"

Don lay sprawling in the sand.

"Tripped over that lazy beast," said Don, picking himself up and aiming a kick at an enormous turtle which was already heading for the water.

"Him bery nice soup making, sar!" cried Spottie, rubbing his brown hands unctuously. But just then a fierce tumult of voices, rolling down from the jungle path, put other thoughts than soup into Spottie's pate.

"The rope! Fetch the rope, Spottie!" cried Jack, throwing himself on the turtle's back.

Don dragged him off.

"Come away!" cried he. "There's no time to fetch that beast along. Are you out of your senses?"

Jack's only reply was to snatch the rope from Spottie's hands, rapidly reeve a running knot at one end, and slip the loop around the body of the giant chelonian, which had by this time reached the water's edge.

All this had occupied much less time than it takes to relate.

The shouts of the mob now sounded ominously near. Without loss of time the canoe was launched, and at once Jack's purpose became apparent.

Seating himself in the bow of the canoe, he drew in the slack of the rope until the turtle was within easy reach, and, holding it firmly so, prodded it with his knife. This was a cruel act, but the stern necessity of the moment outweighed all other considerations.

The turtle at once began making frantic efforts to escape from its tormentor; and as its weight could not have been less than three or four hundred pounds, and its strength in proportion, it easily and rapidly drew the canoe through the water.

In a few minutes they were a stone's throw from shore—and not a moment too soon, for at that instant the mob of natives rushed out of the jungle path, and finding themselves outwitted, gave utterance to a furious howl of disappointment and rage.

The canoe, thanks to the efforts of the turtle, was soon so far from shore that Jack considered it safe to alter their course and steer for the creek. No sooner did he do so than the natives set off at a run in the same direction.

"Dey there canoe got, maybe," observed Spottie, who had now recovered from his fright.

"In that case we may have some fun yet," laughed Jack, lashing the turtle with the rope's end, as if anxious to be in time for the anticipated sport.

By the time the creek was reached, however, not a native was to be seen; so, congratulating themselves on having given their pursuers the slip, they reached the cutter.

Here the old sailor, to say nothing of Puggles, was most anxiously watching for their return.

"Shiver my mizzen!" shouted he, as they ran under the cutter's stern; "ha' ye gone an' took a mermaid in tow, lads?"

"No; one of Spottie's turkles has taken us in tow, captain," replied Jack, setting the turtle free with a slash of his knife, in spite of Spottie's protestations that the creature would make "bery nice soup." "Ugh, you cannibal!" he added, with a glance of disgust at the black's chagrined face, "you wouldn't eat the beast after he has saved your life, would you?"

"Belay there! what's this 'ere yarn about the warmint a-savin' o' your lives, lads?" sang out the captain. "Hours ago," continued he, as the two young men, leaving Spottie to beach the canoe, scrambled on board the cutter, "hours ago I says to myself, 'Mango, my boy,' says I, 'may I never set tooth to salt junk agin if they younkers ain't all dead men afore this,' says I. Howsomedever, here ye be safe an' sound; so let's hear the whole on it, lads."

In compliance with this request Don began to relate the adventures which had befallen them since morning; but scarcely had he got fairly launched upon his narrative, when:

"Sharks an' sea'-sarpents!" interrupted the captain, rising to his feet with a lurch, and pointing up the creek, "what sort o' craft's this 'ere a-bearin' down on us? I axes."

A canoe, laden to the water's edge with natives, appeared round a bend in the creek. Presently other canoes, to the number of half-a-dozen, hove in sight in rapid succession, whose occupants, perceiving their approach to be discovered, set up a shout that made the cliffs ring.

"Spottie was right," cried Jack, catching up a musket, while Don and the captain followed suit; "they've found canoes, and mean to board us."

"Fire my magazine, but we'll give 'em a right warm welcome, then," said the captain. "Look to the primin', lads, an' hold hard when I says fire, for blow me, these 'ere old muskets kicks like a passel o' lubberly donkeys, d'ye see!"

"Captain," Don hastily interposed, "why not draw the bullets and load up with shot? The canoes are so deep in the water that a smart volley of shot right into the midst of the rascals is sure to make them flop over. We've just time to do it."

This suggestion tickled the captain immensely, and without delay the change was made. The canoes were now within easy range.

"Ready, lads," cried the captain:

> "We always be ready,
> Steady, lads, steady!
> We'll fight an' we'll conquer agin and agin!"

Up went the muskets. At sight of them the natives rested on their oars, or rather paddles, and the canoes slowed down.

"Fire!"

The cliffs trembled beneath the treble report. Jack, who in his excitement had forgotten the captain's caution, went sprawling backwards over the thwarts.

"Ho, ho, ho! flint-locks an' small-shot, a

wolley's the thing, lads," roared the captain, pointing up the creek as the smoke rolled away.

"We ne'er see our foes but we wants 'em to stay,
  An' they never see us but they wants us away ;
When they runs, why, we follows an' runs 'em ashore,
For if they won't fight us, we can't do no more !"

The "wolley" had told. Driven frantic by the stinging shot, the natives had leapt to their feet and overturned four out of the seven deeply-laden canoes, whose late occupants were now struggling in the water.

"They've a softer berth of it than I, anyway," said Jack from the bottom of the boat, as he rubbed his shoulder ruefully. "I shall get at the muzzle end of your thundering old blunderbuss next time, captain. Hullo, there's that rascally——"

The remainder of the exclamation was drowned in the creek, for as he uttered it Jack took a header over the stern.

"Shift my ballast, what's the young dog arter now? I axes," cried the captain, gazing aghast at the spot where Jack had disappeared.

His speedy reappearance solved the riddle. By the queue he grasped a dripping, half-naked native, whom he dragged after him to the beach. It was the lascar.

"Hurrah! he's got him this time," shouted Don, leaping out upon the sands to lend a hand in landing the prize.

At first the lascar struggled fiercely for liberty; but as Jack was by no means particular to keep his head above water, he soon quieted down, and presently, with Don's assistance, was hauled out on the sands, where he fell on his knees and began whining piteously for mercy.

"Your revolver, Don," gasped Jack, with a watery side-wink at his friend. "He shall tell us what he knows of the pearls, or die like the dog he is."

Don placed the revolver in his hand, ready cocked. The lascar grovelled in the sand.

"Sa'b, sa'b!" he whined, "you no shoot, me telling anyting."

"No doubt you will," replied Jack significantly, pressing the muzzle of the weapon to his forehead; "but what I want is the truth. Now, then, has old Salambo sold the pearls yet? Come, out with it!"

"He n-n-no selling, sa'b," stammered the

terrified native, shrinking as far away from the pistol as Jack's hold on his queue would permit.

"Where are they, then? Come, look sharp!"

"He d-d-done hiding in Elephant Rock, s-s-sa'b," confessed the lascar, apparently on the point of fainting with terror.

"Don! Captain! Do you hear that?" cried Jack, half-turning, in the excitement produced by this disclosure, towards his friends. "He says old Salambo's hid the pearls in the—— Phew!"

He stopped, with a shrill whistle of dismay. By a quick upward stroke of his arm the lascar had sent the revolver spinning, and at the same instant wrenched himself free from his captor's grasp. Ere Jack could stir hand or foot, he had plunged headlong into the creek.

"Let him go," said Jack tranquilly, as the water closed over the fellow's heels; "we've got an important clue out of him, anyhow."

The captain slowly lowered the musket he had raised for a shot at the fugitive should he come to the surface within range, and said approvingly:

"Right, lad! Spike my guns, I've heard tell as how that 'ere Elephant Rock's riddled from main-deck to keelson, so to say, with gangways, and air-wents, an' sich. Howsomedever, that's matter for arter reflection, as the whale said to himself when he swallied Jonah. The warmints astarn there"—indicating that part of the creek where the occupants of the canoes had taken their involuntary bath — "the warmints astarn ha' sheered off a p'int or two; so now, lads, let's tackle the perwisions afore the wail o' night descends, an' then to work!"

The "wail o' night" was not long in descending, for the sun had disappeared with the lascar. Ere they had done justice to the ample meal which Puggles set before them, and exchanged the draggled pilgrim garb for their everyday clothes, the shadows had crept silently from their hiding-places beneath thicket and cliff, and blotted out the last lingering touch of day from the bosom of the creek. Save the musical chirping of some amorous tree-frog to his mate, or the lazy swish of wings as some belated flying-fox swung slowly past, unbroken silence reigned between the darkling cliffs.

In the captain's opinion, no immediate repetition of the recent attack was to be feared. But the events of the day had made it only too plain·

that their present position was far from being one of security. To remain on board the cutter would be to invite daily skirmishes with the natives, which would not only deter the quest of the golden pearl, but prove a source of constant annoyance and danger.

So far as the captain knew, the island afforded no safer retreat than the hill of the Haunted Pagodas.

The natives of the island, he said, believed this hill to be the abode of a witch in the form of a ferocious tiger, merely to look upon which meant death. For this reason they would on no account venture near it.

So upon the Haunted Pagodas they resolved to fall back without delay. But here an unforeseen difficulty arose.

With the path to the summit of the hill none of the party was acquainted except the captain, and he was unwilling that the precious cutter should be entrusted to the care of any one except himself while the several journeys necessary for the removal of the stores were being made.

"Shiver my main-brace!" roared he, thumping the bottom of the boat with his wooden leg after they had talked it all over. "Shiver my main-brace! I'll go the first trip with ye, lads, an' trust the old cutter to luck."

"See here, captain," said Jack persuasively, "why not trust her to me? It's for only one trip, as you say; and besides, there's not much danger of an attack to-night. You said so yourself."

To this arrangement the old sailor finally agreed. So Don, Spottie, and Puggles loaded up with the stores and other necessaries for their proposed sojourn on the summit of the hill, and a start was made, the captain leading with musket and lantern.

"Good-bye, Jack!" Don called back, as he struck into the jungle at the captain's heels. "Fire a gun if you want help."

"All right, old fellow," was Jack's careless reply. "Good-bye till I see you again!"

So, with no other companion than Bosin, he was left alone to guard the cutter.

And now the difficulties of the captain's party began in earnest. The path before them was, it is true, scarce half a mile in length, but so precipitous was the hillside, so overgrown the track, that every furlong seemed a league. The tangled, overhanging jungle growth not only completely shut out the rays of the moon, but by its thickness impeded their progress at every step, as though determined to guard the abode of the witch-tiger from all human intrusion. To make matters worse, they had neglected to provide themselves with an axe.

"Shiver my main-brace!" the captain cried, as his wooden leg stuck fast in a tangled mass of creepers. "These 'ere land trips be a pesky sight worse nor a sea woyage, says you! Blow me! I'd ruther round the Horn in mid-winter than wade through such wegetation as this 'ere in midnight darkness! Howsomedever, the port's afore us, so up we goes, as Jonah says to the whale when he bid the warmint adoo."

Up they went accordingly, and after much stumbling and tough climbing, reached the summit and the Haunted Pagodas. Finding here a clear space and bright moonlight, they quickly relieved themselves of their loads.

"An' now, lads," cried the captain, "wear ship an' back to the cutter, says you. Fire my magazine! what's that? I axes."

Sharp and distinct upon the night air there floated up from the darkness of the ravine the report of a gun.

Don felt his heart stand still with dread, then race at lightning speed.

"An attack!" he cried hoarsely; "and Jack alone! Hurry, captain!—for God's sake hurry!"

Easier said than done. Haste only added to the difficulties of the way. It seemed to Don that he should never shake off the retarding clutch of the jungle.

At last their weary feet pressed again the sands of the little beach. But now a new terror seized them. The beach was illuminated by a ruddy, fitful glow. The cutter was on fire!

Don cleared the sands almost at a bound.

"Jack!" he shouted, leaping the cutter's rail, and with lightning glance scanning the bottom of the boat, and then the cuddy, for some sign of his friend. "Jack, where are you? Captain, he's not here! and—my God! look at this!"

Upon the bottom of the boat, showing darkly crimson in the ruddy firelight, lay a pool of blood, and beside it a discharged musket.

CHAPTER VIII.

AT THE HAUNTED PAGODAS.

The fire, fortunately, had gained so little headway that a few bucketfuls of water sufficed to put the *Jolly Tar* out of danger. Then the captain stumped up to Don, where he sat disconsolate on the cutter's gun'le, and laid a sympathetic hand upon his shoulder.

"Cheer up, my hearty! They warmints ain't done for Master Jack yet, not by a long chalk, says I. Flush my scuppers, lad!" he roared in stentorian tones, as he turned the light of the lantern upon the pool of blood, "this 'ere sanguinary gore as dyes the deck bain't his'n at all. It's the blood o' some native warmint, what he's gone an' let daylight into, d'ye mind me, an' here's the musket as done the trick."

"Then you think he's not—not dead?" asked Don, steadying his voice with an effort.

"Dead? Not him! Alive he is, and alive he remains," cried the old sailor. "An' why so? you naterally axes. To begin with, as the shark says when he nipped the seaman's leg off, because the keg o' powder's gone. Spurts, the warmints thinks to theirselves, an' so they makes away with it. Secondly"—and here the old sailor's voice grew husky—"because that 'ere imp of a Bosin's gone. 'I'll stand hard by Master Jack,' says he, so off *he* goes. Sharks an' sea-sarpents, lad, can't ye see as the lubbers have only gone an' took Master Jack in tow?"

"But I can't understand," persisted Don, "why they should do it."

"Ransom, lad, that's what the lubbers is arter. Master Jack's life's worth a sight more'n a bag o' pearls, an' well they knows it.

> "Avast there, an' don't be a milksop so soft,
> To be taken for trifles aback;
> There's a Providence, lad, as sits up aloft
> To watch for the life of poor Jack.'

Trolling out this sailorly reproof of Don's fears, the captain stretched himself in the bottom of the boat, and drawing a tarpaulin over his nose, was soon sleeping off the effects of his recent exertions ashore. But upon Don's heart his chum's fate lay like a leaden weight. He could not rest.

"Good-bye, old fellow, till I see you again." These, Jack's last careless words, repeated themselves in every mournful sigh of the night-wind; and as he lay, hour after hour, watching the stars climb the heavens, he wondered, with a keen pain at his heart, when that "again" was to be.

As the night wore on, however, he found more and more comfort in the old sailor's words. It was so much easier to believe that Jack had been kidnapped than to believe him dead. This view of his disappearance, too, was altogether in keeping with the shark-charmer's cunning. As for himself, he would gladly have cried quits with old Salambo then and there, if by so doing he could have recalled Jack to his side.

At length he fell into a troubled sleep, unconscious of the fact that another brain than his was busy with Jack's fate. Had he but known it, Bosin deserved more than a passing thought that night.

By daybreak they were again astir, and within an hour the cutter lay snugly ensconced in the shelter of a deep, vine-draped cavern beneath the cliff, some hundred yards down the creek, of which the captain knew. In carrying out this part of the old sailor's plan, the canoe, for which an effective paddle was improvised out of an old oar, proved of signal service; and when the smaller skiff had in its turn been hidden away in the dense jungle bordering the beach, they loaded up with the remaining stores, and took the pathway to the Haunted Pagodas, which they eventually reached just as the sun, like a huge ball of fire, rolled up out of the eastern sea.

As the captain had said, the Haunted Pagodas was indeed "a tidy spot to fall back upon." Ages before, a circle of massive temples had crowned the summit of this island hill; but for full a thousand years had Nature searched out with silent, prying fingers the minutest crevices of the closely-cemented stones, ruthlessly destroying what man had so proudly reared, until nothing save a confusion of tumble-down walls and broken pillars, grotesquely draped with climbing vines and like parasitic growths, remained to mark the site of the erstwhile stately cloisters. A shuddery spot it was!—a likely lurking-place for reptile or wild beast, so uncanny in its weird union of jungle wildness and dead men's work, that one would scarcely have been surprised had the terrible witch-tiger of the native legend suddenly leapt out upon one from some dark pit or sunless recess.

In one spot alone had the walls successfully resisted the action of the insinuating roots. This was a sort of cloister with a floor of stone, upon which the roof had fallen. But when the *débris* had been cleared away, and the stores scattered about in its stead, this corner of the ruins looked positively homelike and comfortable — especially when Puggles, taking possession of one of its angles, converted it into a kitchen, and began active preparations for breakfast. The captain dubbed their new retreat " the fo'csle."

All that day the old sailor was in an unusually thoughtful mood. Every half-hour or so he would produce his pipe and take a number of slow, meditative " whiffs o' the fragrant," after which he would slap his thigh energetically with one horny hand, and stump back and forth amid the ruins in a state of high excitement, until, something going wrong with his train of thought, the pipe had to be relighted, and the difficulty, like the tobacco, smoked out again.

This characteristic process of " ilin' up his runnin' gear " he continued far on into the afternoon, when he abruptly laid the huge meerschaum aside, took a critical survey of sea and sky, and, bearing down on Don, where he sat cleaning the muskets, without further ado planted a resounding thump on that young gentleman's back.

"Blow me!" he burst out, as if Don was already initiated into his train of thought, "the wery identical thing, lad. An' what's that? you naterally axes. Why, d'ye see, I've been splicin' o' my idees together a bit, so to say, an' shiver my main-brace if I ain't gone an' rescued Master Jack!"

Edging away a little lest the captain's rising excitement should again culminate in one of his well-meant, but none the less undesirable thumps, "You mean, I suppose," said Don, "that you've hit upon a plan for his rescue."

"Ay, lad," assented the captain, "but an idee well spun is a deed half done, d'ye mind me. Howsomedever, let's take our bearin's afore we runs for port, says you. An' to begin with, as the shark said——"

What the shark said, as well as what the captain was about to say, was doomed to remain for ever a matter of conjecture, for at that instant Puggles set up a shout that effectually interrupted the conversation.

"Sa'b! sar! me done see um, sa'b. Him done come back, sar."

Naturally enough, Don's first thought was of Jack. He sprang to his feet, his heart giving a wild leap of joy, and then standing still with suspense. For in all the clearing no human form appeared.

Puggles had now reached his master's side. "Him there got, sa'b, there!" he reiterated, pointing towards the narrow break in the jungle which indicated the starting-point of the pathway to the creek. Between this point and the spot where they stood, the jungle grass grew thick and tall. As they looked they saw it sway in a long, wavy undulation, as if some living thing were rapidly making its way towards them. In another moment the rank covert parted, and there appeared, not Jack, but Bosin.

"Knots an' marlinspikes!" ejaculated the delighted captain, as the monkey scrambled chattering upon his knee. "What's this 'ere as the imp o' darkness's been an' made a prize of? I axes."

Around the monkey's neck a shred of draggled, blood-stained linen was securely bound. Already Don was fumbling at the knot, his face whiter than the rag itself.

"A message from Jack!" he announced joyfully, when at length the tightly-drawn knot yielded, and a scrap of paper fluttered to the ground.

"Shiver my main-brace!" roared the captain, bringing his hand down on that unoffending member as if about to give a practical demonstration of his words, "ain't I said as much all along, lad? Alive he is, an' alive he remains. An' blow me if ever I see anything to beat this 'ere method o' excommunicating atween friends, says I. So let's hear what Master Jack has got to say for hisself."

Don had already run his eye over the pencilled writing. "He's all right, thank God!" he exclaimed, in a tone of intense relief. "Wounded, as I feared—a mere scratch, he says—but you shall hear for yourself:—

"'Don't be cut up, old fellow,'" he read aloud, "'it will all come right in the end. The niggers pounced down on me before I heard them. Just had time to let off one of the captain's old kickers, when a crack on the head laid me out. I'm in a village on the sea-shore, and by great good luck I can see the hill and the smoke of what, I suppose, is your fire, from the window of the hut they've stuck me in. It doesn't seem quite so bad when I look at that. . . . Bosin just turned up. Am writing in hopes he'll carry this safely to you. Close prisoner. Have to scribble when the beggars aren't watching me. Overheard them palavering just now. They take me to the E. R. to-night—'"

"Which he means the Elephant Rock!" cried the captain, interrupting. "Blow me! I knowed as that 'ere Elephant 'ud go an' make wittles of him, d'ye see?"

Don nodded and read on:

"'Old Salambo's work this. He means to make terms for the pearls——'"

"Copper my bottom, lad! Them's the wery identical words as I've stood by all along!" the captain broke in again.

"Wait!" said Don impatiently. "There's something important here. I couldn't make it out before, the writing's so scrawly towards the end. Listen to this: 'There's a streak down the face of the hill, that looks like a path to the village here. If Bosin's in time, come early. Don't let the hdkf. alarm you; it's a mere scratch.'"

Reading off these last words rapidly, Don

pointed to the sun, already half-hidden by the western horizon.

"There's no time to lose, captain! He must be set free before he's taken to the Rock."

"Right, lad; so let's tumble out and man the guns!" cried the captain, lurching to his feet and giving his pantaloons a determined hitch-up.

"We always be ready!
Steady, lad, steady!
We'll fight an' we'll conquer agin and agin!"

"That we will," assented Don heartily; "but first we must get the bearings of this village, captain. Where's the glass? Spottie! Hi, Spottie!—the glass here!"

In response to the summons, Puggles ran up with the captain's telescope.

"Spottie done go fetch water, sa'b," he explained.

"There is a village," Don announced, after adjusting the instrument and carefully sweeping the sea-shore. "Just there, in that clump of trees; the only one within range, so far as I can see. Do you make it out, captain?"

"Ay," said the captain, taking the glass; "there's a willage below, sure as sharks is sharks."

"The next thing, then," continued Don, "is to

find this path Jack speaks of. 'Twould take us two good hours at least to go round by way of the creek. Do you know, I've a notion the path to the spring is the one we want. Suppose we try it?"

The captain making no demur, Don caught up a musket and led the way to the spring. This spring was Spottie's discovery. It lay to the left of the creek path, about fifty yards down the hillside. The jungle had almost obliterated the path by which it was approached, but this the black had in some degree remedied by a vigorous use of the axe during the day, and, as Puggles had intimated, he was now at the spring, replenishing the water bucket.

Hardly had Don and the captain got fairly into the path when there rose from the depths of the jungle immediately below them a series of frantic yells. The voice was undoubtedly Spottie's, and, judging from the manner in which he used it, Spottie stood—or believed he stood—in sore need of assistance. Quickening his pace to a run, Don soon came upon him, making for the open, minus bucket and turban, his eyes protruding from their sockets, and altogether in a terrible state of fright.

"What's the matter?" cried Don, catching him by the arm and shaking him until he was fain to cease his bellowing.

"De t-t-tiger-witch, sa'b!" said Spottie, his teeth chattering. "Me done see um, sa'b!"

Just then the captain came up.

"He's seen a monkey or something, and thinks it's the tiger-witch," explained Don, laughing at the poor fellow's piteous face. "Whereabouts is it, Spottie?"

Spottie pointed fearfully down the shadowy pathway, where a faint snapping of twigs could be heard in the underbrush.

"Blow me!" said the captain, after listening intently a moment, "yon warmint bain't no monkey, lad. So let's lay alongside an' diskiver what quarter o' the animile kingdom he hails from, says you."

And with that he started off in the direction of the sound.

Bidding Spottie remain where he was, Don followed. The captain was, perhaps, ten paces in advance. Suddenly the jungle parted with a loud swish, and a tawny body shot through the air and alighted full upon the captain's back, bearing him to the ground ere he could utter so much as a cry.

Don stood petrified. Then a savage, guttural growling, accompanied by a sickening crunching sound, roused him to the old sailor's danger. There was just sufficient light left to show the two figures on the ground—the tiger atop, his fangs buried in the captain's thigh. Priming the musket rapidly with some loose powder he happened to have in his pocket, Don sprang to the captain's aid. The tiger lifted its head at his approach with an angry snarl, but this was no time to think of his own danger. Quick as thought he thrust the muzzle of the musket between the beast's jaws and fired.

An instant later and he was on his back. The tiger had sprung clean over him, knocking him down in its passage, and now lay some yards away, writhing in the death struggle. Don picked himself up and ran to the old sailor's side. As he reached the spot where he lay, the captain struggled into a sitting posture, and stared about him bewilderedly.

"Stave my bulkhead!" roared he, "if this bain't the purtiest go as ever I see. An' what quarter o' the animile kingdom might the warmint hail from? I axes."

"A tiger, captain; a genuine man-eater. But, I say, are you hurt?"

"Hurt is it?" demanded the captain. "Why, d'ye see, lad," first adjusting his neckcloth, and then proceeding to feel himself carefully over, "barrin' this 'ere bit of a chafe to my figgerhead, I hain't started a nail, d'ye see. Avast there! Shiver my main-brace, what's this? I axes."

Just where the "main-brace" was spliced upon the thigh, a sad rent in the captain's broad pantaloons showed the wooden portion of his anatomy to be deeply indented and splintered. At this discovery he stopped aghast in the process of feeling for broken bones.

"Why, don't you see how it is?" laughed Don. "The brute has tried to make a meal off your wooden leg, captain."

The captain burst into one of his tremendous guffaws. "Blow me if I don't admire the warmint's taste," said he. "An uncommon affectionate un he is, says you, so let's pay our respec's to him 'ithout delay, lad."

The tiger proved to be a magnificent specimen of his tribe; and, as he stood over the tawny carcase in the waning light, Don could not repress a feeling of pardonable pride at thought of his own share in the adventure which had ended so disastrously for the superb creature at his feet.

"Captain," said he presently, when that worthy had inspected and admired the striped monster to his heart's content, "captain, it strikes me as being somewhat of a rare thing to run against a full-blown tiger on an island like this. Don't you think so?"

"Ay, that it is," assented the captain; "rare as sea-sarpents."

"That explains it, then: the tiger-witch story, I mean. This chap's great size, and the fact that man-eaters aren't often met with on these little nutshell islands, have made him the terror of the whole community, you see. He's their witch, I'll be bound. Now;" he ran on, seeing the captain express his approval of this likely explanation by a series of emphatic nods, "now I'll tell you what I mean to do. Dear old Jack's a prisoner, and we're bound to get him out of limbo if we can. His captors—those native beggars—go in mortal terror of this beast here. Good! Why shouldn't Pug and I carry the creature's skin down to the village yonder—where Jack is, you know—use it to impersonate the witch-tiger, and terrify the niggers——"

He got no farther with his explanation, for the captain, having already grasped the idea, at this point grasped its originator by the hand, and cut in with: "Spike my guns, the wery identical thing, lad! Blow me, the lubberly swabs'll tumble into the jungle like a lot o' porpoises when they sees that 'ere tiger-skin a-hangin' on your recreant limbs. An' then hooray for Master Jack, says you! Why not? I axes."

CHAPTER IX.

WAS IT JACK?

WHAT a night it was! Overhead one glorious maze of scintillating stars; in the jungle ebon blackness, shot with the soft glow of myriad fireflies, that flashed their tiny lamps only to leave the spot they had illumined more intensely black than before.

Don's surmise as to the spring path proved correct—it extended quite to the foot of the hill, where it merged almost imperceptibly into the scantier vegetation fringing the sea-shore. After a hard fight with the difficulties of the way—increased in no small degree by the dead weight of the tiger-skin—he and Puggles at length reached the limits of the jungle and paused for breath. The utmost caution was now necessary in order to avoid untimely discovery.

The moon was not yet up, and the cocoa-nut

tope in which, but a stone's throw away, nestled the village that formed at once their destination and Jack's place of imprisonment, lay wrapped in gloom so impenetrable that not a single outline of tree or hut could be distinguished from where they stood. Excepting a faint glow, which at infrequent intervals flickered amid the lofty branches of the palm-trees, there was nothing to show that the spot was tenanted by any human being. This light— or, to speak more correctly, this reflection of a light — Don attributed to a fire in the village street.

"They done lighting um for company, maybe," suggested Puggles. "Plenty people going feast, black man 'fraid got, making fire keep tiger-witch off."

"So much the better for us," said his master; "especially if everybody's at the town except the fellows in charge of Jack. But shut up, Pug; it won't do to risk their overhearing our palaver."

With stealthy steps they advanced, pausing often to listen, until they gained the deeper shade of the trees close under the rear of the huts. Leaving the black boy here, Don skirted the nearer row of cabins and took a cautious view of the street.

The huts stood in two irregular rows, one facing the other, and midway down the open space or street between was a smouldering fire of brushwood, about which, in listless, drowsy attitudes, there lolled a group of perhaps twenty natives. Save for these the place, so far as he could make out, was quite deserted. The doors of the huts were closed, and no glimmer of lamp or fire shone through them to indicate that any occupants were within. A little to one side of the fire the light fell upon an object at sight of which Don started violently. It was the stolen keg of powder. Jack could not be far off, then!

Quitting the spot as noiselessly as he had approached it, he made his way back to the rear of the huts, and with the assistance of Puggles, adjusted the limp tiger's pelt upon his back, shoulders, and head. Next he gave the black boy his orders. He was to lie close until the natives about the fire took to flight—which, if they fled at all, would, in the ordinary course of events, be in the direction of the other extremity of the street—when he was to join his master in searching the huts.

All was now in readiness, and Don, gripping the defunct tiger's ears at either side of his head to hold the skin in position, once more skirted the row of huts, Puggles in close attendance. His former post of observation gained, he went down upon all-fours, and when Puggles had readjusted the skin to his satisfaction, in this attitude he boldly advanced into the street.

The distance to be traversed in order to reach the group about the fire was not less than fifty yards. He had covered a third of the ground unobserved, when one of the natives rose to his feet and threw a fresh bundle of faggots on the smouldering embers. Fanned by the breeze, the fire blazed up fiercely, illuminating the street from end to end. The tiger-witch uttered a terrific roar.

When this sound fell upon the ears of the native, he wheeled and peered fearfully into the semi-darkness in which Don's end of the street lay. A second roar brought a second native to his feet. He was followed by another and another, till all were on the alert. The witch-tiger was now in full view.

For a little while the group about the fire hesitated. Should they stand their ground or decamp? As the intruder advanced, and the ruddy firelight threw its gruesome outlines into stronger relief, they suddenly perceived what manner of apparition this was that had stolen upon them out of the darkness. To them the tiger-witch, with its swift, silent visitations of death, had doubtless long been a dread reality. The island held but one tiger—and here it was! With frantic outcries they turned and fled pell-mell down the village street.

This was just what Don desired—what he had calculated upon. Until the heels of the hindermost had quite disappeared in the darkness, he sustained his rôle. Thus far the ruse had succeeded admirably. But the real business of the night had as yet only begun. Shaking the clammy skin from off his back, he rose to his feet and made a dash for the door of the nearest hut. Just as he reached it, Puggles, who had watched the rout of the natives with shaking sides, came trotting up.

"Look alive, Pug!" cried his master, bursting in the frail door with a crash. "Search the huts on the left, while I take these on the right. Look alive, I say—they may come back at any minute."

Puggles needed no urging. He was only too well aware of the danger that threatened his master and his own precious self should the fugitives think better of their cowardice and reappear on the scene. He set to work with a will.

Into hut after hut they forced their way, peering into every nook and corner, and calling upon Jack as loudly as they dared; only to receive for answer the dull echoes of their own shouts. Nowhere was there any sign of Jack. "Had he been already removed?" Don asked himself desperately, as he sped from door to door. It almost seemed so; but while a single hut remained unsearched there was still hope.

Half-a-dozen only were left, when the catastrophe he had all along been dreading actually occurred. The natives came trooping back. To their infinite relief, no doubt, the witch-tiger had vanished, and in its stead appeared two human figures darting from hut to hut. The natives raised a shout of defiance and pressed forward to the attack, catching up as weapons whatever came first to hand.

Crossing the street at a bound, Don joined the black boy, just as the latter emerged from the doorway of a hut, and thrust into his hands one of two pistols with which he had come provided. Backing against the door of the hut, with pistols drawn they awaited the attack. It began with a rattling volley of missiles, but the low, projecting thatch of the native dwelling, jutting out as it did several feet from the wall, served to somewhat break the force of the stony hail.

"Don't fire till I give the word," said Don between his teeth. "We can't afford to waste a shot. The beggars are drawing their knives."

The words had barely left his lips when, with a shout and a disorderly rush, the crowd broke for the spot where they stood.

"Ready, Pug. Fire!"

Simultaneously with the sharp crack of the pistols, there leapt skyward from mid-street a sudden, blinding flash of lurid light, accompanied by dense volumes of sulphurous smoke, and a thunderous shock that shook the walls of the huts to their foundations. Don and his companion were dashed violently through the door against which they stood, and hurled upon the floor within. A thick shower of sand and stones rattled about and upon them. But of this fact they were unconscious. The shock had stunned them.

When Don came to himself he found Puggles seated on the ground by his side, blubbering dismally.

"What's the matter? Where are the natives?" he demanded, struggling to his feet, and scanning the interior of the hut with bewildered eyes. "Hullo, the roof's on fire!"

Not only was the roof ablaze, but showers of

THE EXPLOSION.

glowing sparks fell thickly upon them. The floor of the hut was a bed of fire, the heat intolerable. Puggles, dazed by the recent shock, and stupefied with fright, seemed to comprehend not a word that was said to him. Don accordingly seized him by the arm and dragged him into the street.

Here the scene was appalling indeed. How long he had lain insensible he could not tell; but the time thus spent upon the floor of the hut must have been considerable, for from end to end the double line of thatched dwellings was wrapped in flames that shot high into the inky air, and there united in one roaring, swirling canopy of fire above the narrow thoroughfare. As if to render the spectacle more awful, here and there lay stretched upon the ground the mangled, blackened body of a native. Through one of these a sharp splinter of wood had been driven. Don examined it curiously. Then—he had been too dazed to realise it before—the truth flashed upon him. The keg of powder had exploded!

Whilst crossing the street to Pug's side he had noticed, he remembered now, that the head of the keg was stove in. It then lay close beside the fire, within a few feet of the scene of the attack. It was not there now, but in its stead was a shallow, blackened cavity. That told the whole story of the explosion. A handful of powder carelessly scattered, a wisp of straw kicked into the fire amid the rush of feet, a chance spark even, and——

"Sa'b, sa'b, the huts done tumble in!"

Puggles was tugging at his sleeve, and pointing fearfully down the street. For an instant Don gazed into the black boy's face blankly, not grasping the import of his words. Then, like a repetition of that lurid flash of light which had burnt itself into his very brain, came the recollection of Jack.

The sudden return of the natives had left but half-a-dozen huts unsearched. These were situated at the extreme end of the street—the end opposite to that from which Don and Puggles had approached the village. Towards these the former now ran, only to discover, to his consternation, that the fire was before him. For in this direction the wind blew, and the unsearched huts, like the rest, were a seething mass of flames. Of all save one the roofs had already given way, while at the very moment he ran up that also crashed in.

As the blood-red flames shot skyward, an agonised, inarticulate shriek rose from within the glowing walls.

Was it Jack?

Shielding his face with his hands, Don attempted to force an entrance, but the heat of the furnace-like doorway drove him back. In frantic accents he called his chum by name—called again and again—to be answered only by the hissing of the pitiless flame-tongues that licked the black heavens.

Was it Jack? Had the natives who escaped —if, indeed, any did—the deadly effects of the explosion, carried him with them in their flight from the burning village, or had he been mercilessly abandoned to a fiery grave within his prison walls?

It was a terrible question; but not that night, nor for many nights to come, was he to know whether those unnumbered moments of unconsciousness had consigned his chum to continued captivity or to death.

One thing only was certain: their mission to the village had reached a disastrous climax. To remain longer where they were was useless; to follow the trail of the natives who had escaped, impossible. No course was left but immediate return to the camp.

Weary, dejected, with aching bodies and aching hearts — for even light-hearted Puggles, heathen though he was, felt crushed by their sad misadventure — they sought the spot where the axe and lantern had been left, and then set their blackened faces towards the hill.

By this time the moon had risen, making the task of finding the footpath an easy one. Just as they turned their backs upon the beach and the burning village, out upon the tense stillness of the night — a stillness softened rather than broken by the music of the surf — from the shadowy hill above rang the sharp report of a gun.

"Something wrong up there, I'm afraid," said Don, rousing himself and pausing to listen. "Hullo!" as a second report broke the stillness, "there goes another! Come, Pug, we must pull ourselves together a bit and get over the ground faster. The captain's not a man to waste powder; those reports mean danger."

"Him maybe another lubberly warmint shooting, sa'b," Pug suggested.

"Unless I'm very much mistaken, there's something a jolly sight worse afoot," was his master's uneasy rejoinder as they began the ascent.

Here and there upon the hillside were spots where the rains of many summers had so washed away the thin surface-soil as to lay bare the rock beneath and leave little or no roothold for vegetation. As he paused for a brief breathing space

K

in one of these clearings, Don's attention was drawn to a dull red glare, which, though but a short distance in advance of the spot where he stood, had up to that moment been quite concealed by the intervening jungle.

"Say, Pug, what do you make of that light?"

The black boy knuckled his eyes vigorously, as if to assure himself they were playing him no trick.

"Me tinking there one fire got, sa'b," said he, after a long look at the mysterious light.

"In that case we'd better stir our stumps. The breeze seems to be freshening, and once the fire gets a hold on this tindery jungle, why, there's no knowing——"

"There another got, sa'b!" broke in Puggles, pointing excitedly to the right.

"Phew! And, by Jove, there's a third beyond that again! And the wind's blowing straight for the camp, too! Now I understand why the captain fired those shots! The hill's on fire! Point, Pug!"

Up the hillside they bounded, panting, stumbling. There was light enough now and to spare, for the fire towards which they were advancing had made more headway than at first sight appeared. The wonder was that they had not observed it sooner; but this perhaps was sufficiently accounted for by the fact that the thoughts of both had lagged behind in the burning village.

The point of danger was soon reached. The fire had not yet crossed the path, but only a few yards of tindery underbrush separated the swaying wall of flame-shot smoke from the narrow trail, while every instant the margin grew perceptibly less.

"Now for it, Pug!"

Don raced past with head lowered, the greedy flames licking his face. Half-blinded, he stumbled on for a dozen yards or so before turning to ascertain how Puggles had stood the ordeal. To his horror he then discovered that the fire had swallowed up the pathway at a single bound, and that Puggles was nowhere to be seen.

CHAPTER X.

IN WHICH THE OLD SAW, "OUT OF THE FRYING-PAN, INTO THE FIRE," IS REVERSED WITH STARTLING EFFECT.

BACK he ran, battling with the flames and sparks that rolled in volumes up the hillside, until, half-stifled and well-nigh fainting from the heat, he was forced to turn and flee for his life before the swiftly advancing flames.

Whether Puggles, terrified by the close proximity of the fire, had hung back at the last moment, or whether he had attempted to follow his master and paid for his devotion with his life, heaven alone knew.

"Poor chap!" gasped Don, as he stumbled free of the smoke and turned for a last look at the fiery veil so suddenly drawn over his faithful servant's fate. "God help him!"

The rapid advance of the fire, however, allowed

little time for the indulgence of emotion. The long rainless months had scorched the face of the hill until the thick-set bamboo copse was as dry as tinder, inflammable as shavings. The wind and the steepness of the hillside, too, proved powerful allies of the flames. On and up they swept, leaping from point to point with such rapidity that Don found it necessary to strain every nerve to avoid being overtaken by the greedy holocaust. Glad indeed was he when, the scene of his recent adventure passed, he at length emerged upon the comparatively open ground abreast of the encampment.

Stumping uneasily to and fro, "abaft the fo'csle," with Bosin perched contentedly upon his shoulder, was the old sailor—the jerky creak, creak of his wooden leg showing him to be in an unusually disturbed state of mind.

"Right glad I am to clap eyes on ye, lad!" he sang out cheerily on catching sight of the returned wanderer. "An' whereaway's Master Jack an' the leetle nigger, I axes?"

The captain paused abruptly, both in his walk and speech, for the pained look on Don's blackened but ghastly face told him at a glance that something more than ordinary was amiss.

Slowly setting down the lantern, which he had all along retained in his grasp—most fortunately, as it turned out—Don threw himself on the trampled grass, and, as rapidly as his shortness of breath would permit, summed up the disastrous results of his village expedition. In open-mouthed silence, as was his wont, the old sailor listened; but when he learned of the dark uncertainty that overhung the fate of Jack and Puggles, he hastily brushed aside a tear that straggled down his weather-beaten cheek, and, in a voice husky with emotion, burst into one of his characteristic snatches of song:

> "Why, what's that to you if my eyes I'm a-wipin'?
>   A tear is a pleasure, d'ye see, in its way.
> 'Tis nonsense for trifles, I owns, to be pipin',
>   But they as hain't pity—why, I pities they!"

And having delivered himself of this sailorly apology for his weakness, he added in his usual voice:

"Blow me!—as the speakin' trumpet says to the skipper—if ever I hear'd any yarn as beats this 'un, lad. Howsomedever, when the ship's a-sinkin', pipin' your eye ain't a-goin' to stop the leak, d'ye mind me; an' so, just to bear away on the off tack a bit, what d'ye make o' this 'ere conflecgration, I axes?"

"I can tell you better what it came jolly near making of me, captain, and that's cinders! But what do *you* make of it?—and, by the way, what were those shots for? You don't think there's any danger here, do you?"

"Ay," replied the captain, with an emphatic tug at his neckerchief, "that I does, lad! An' why? you naterally axes. Because, d'ye mind me, the hill's ablaze from stem to starn—blow me if it bain't! Howsomedever," leading the way towards a jagged remnant of wall that stood out in ghostly solitude amid the ruins, "go aloft an' cast an eye out to lee'ard, lad."

The captain's ominous words prepared Don for an unpleasant surprise; yet, when he had scaled the pile of masonry, an involuntary cry of alarm broke from him.

"Good heavens, captain, we're surrounded by fire!"

"Right, lad! an' the confleegration's gettin' uncommon clost under our weather bow, says you. An hour back, d'ye see, I sights the first on 'em alongside o' the path below, an' fires the gun to signal ye to put about. An' then, flush my scuppers! what does I see but a hull sarcle o' confleegrations, as it may be a cable's len'th apart, clean round the hill, lad! an' so I fires the second wolley."

"This is the work of those cowardly niggers!" said Don, clenching his fists. "They daren't come here to fight us, so they mean to scorch us out!"

"The wery identical words as I says to myself when first I sights the fires, lad," rejoined the captain; "an' a purty lot o' tobackie it cost me afore I overhauled the idee, says you."

"It's likely to cost us more than a few pipes of tobacco, I'm afraid, captain," said Don uneasily, leaping down from his post of observation. "The fire's close upon us, and once this grass catches, why, good-bye to the stores! I say, where's Spottie?"

"Belay there!" chuckled the captain, who, somehow, seemed remarkably cheerful, considering the gravity of the situation. "Whereaway's the nigger, you axes? Why, d'ye mind me, lad, this 'ere old hulk ain't been a-lyin' on her beam-ends all this time, not by a long chalk. The nigger's with the stores, d'ye see; an' stow my cargo, where should the stores be but safe and snug under hatches?"

With that he seized his perplexed companion by the arm, skirted the dilapidated wall, and presently halted on the very brink of a black chasm that yawned to the stars close under its rear. Little else was to be seen, for the wall cut off the light of both the fire and the moon. From the depths of the cavity proceeded a sound suspiciously like snoring. The captain indulged in another chuckle, and then, shaping his hands into a sort of speaking-trumpet, he bent over the hole and shouted loudly for Spottie. The snoring suddenly ceased, and in half a minute or so up the black tumbled, rubbing his eyes. The captain bade him fetch the lantern, adding strict injunctions that he should replenish the store of oil before lighting it.

"And now, lad, let's go below," said he, when Spottie had fulfilled his mission.

So down they went, the captain leading. First came a dozen or more moss-grown steps, littered with blocks of stone, which, ages before, perhaps, had fallen and found a resting-place here. At the foot of the steps there opened out a subterranean passage, of height sufficient to admit of Don's standing erect in it with ease. Upon the floor lay the stores; beyond these again all was blank darkness. To all appearance the passage extended far into the bowels of the hill.

"Blow me!" chuckled the captain, turning a triumphant gaze upon the massive walls, "electric lightnin' itself ud never smell us out in sich a tidy berth as this, says you."

"It certainly is a snug spot," assented Don; "though I wish"—glancing round at their sadly depleted numbers—"I wish that Jack and Pug were as safe, poor fellows."

"Cheer up, my hearty. As I says afore, 'there's a Providence, lad, as sits up aloft to keep watch for the life of poor Jack.' Ay, an' for the nigger's too, d'ye mind me, lad," rejoined the captain, blowing his nose loudly. "So let's turn out an' see what manner o' headway the conflecgration's makin'."

Brief as was their absence from "the glimpses of the moon," the fire had made alarming progress in the interval. Viewed from the centre of the swiftly-narrowing cordon of flame, the scene was awesome in the extreme. The rear column of the invader advanced the more slowly of the two, but even it was now within a stone's throw of that godsend, the captain's "tidy berth."

On the seaward side the flames had overleapt

the jungle's edge, and seized with unsated greed upon the luxuriant grass that everywhere grew amid the ruins. Nearer still, the dense, parasitic growth upon the remnant of wall, ignited by the dense clouds of sparks which the wind drove far ahead of the actual fire, was blazing fiercely. The heat was stifling; the air, choked with smoke and showers of glowing sparks, unbreathable. They retreated precipitately to the cooler shelter of the underground chamber.

Even here the noise of the flames could be distinctly heard. Indeed, they had been barely ten minutes below when the fiery sea rolled with a sullen roar over their heads, the fierce heat driving them back from the entrance.

Some hours must pass before it would be either safe or practicable to venture into the open air. Accordingly, following the captain's example, Don made himself as comfortable for the night as circumstances permitted. A quantity of dried grass, which Spottie had thoughtfully collected and deposited beside the stores, afforded an excellent bed, and soon the deep breathing of all three told that sleep too had made this long untenanted nook her refuge.

Upwards of an hour had passed when a tremendous grinding crash shook the passage from roof to floor, and brought Don and the captain to their feet. They had fallen asleep surrounded by a subdued glow of firelight; they woke to find themselves in pitchy darkness. Bosin and the scarcely more courageous Spottie began to whimper.

"Avast there!" the captain sang out at the latter. "Is this a time to begin a-pipin' of your eye like a wench, I axes? Belay that, ye lubberly swab, an' light the binnacle lamp till we takes our bearin's."

This order Spottie obeyed with an alacrity which, it is but due to him to explain, sprang rather from a dread of his master's heavy boot than from his fear of the dark. In the light thus thrown on the situation, the cause of the recent crash became only too apparent. So, too, did its effect.

The ruined wall which overtopped their place of refuge had fallen, completely blocking the exit with huge stones, still glowing hot from the action of the fire.

"Batten—my—hatches, lad!" ejaculated the old sailor, as the full significance of the catastrophe flashed upon him. "We're prisoners, says you!"

CHAPTER XI.

INTO THE HEART OF THE HILL.

THERE was no denying the truth of the captain's disconcerting announcement. So far as concerned the ancient flight of steps, egress from the underground chamber was wholly cut off. In the space of a single moment their refuge had become a prison. For, to begin with, the stones which blocked the entrance were glowing hot; while, to end with, these were of such a size, and so tightly wedged between the walls of the narrow opening, as to render any attempt at removing them, in the absence of suitable implements, utterly futile. If ever there existed a dilemma worthy the consumption of the captain's tobacco, here was one. The huge meerschaum was lighted forthwith.

And never, perhaps, in all its long and varied history, did the pipe perform its task of "'ilin' up" the old sailor's "runnin' gear" so promptly and satisfactorily as now. For scarcely had he taken half-a-dozen "whiffs o' the fragrant," when, "Blow me, lad!" he exclaimed, triumphantly following with the stem of the pipe the course of a blue spiral which had just left his lips, "d'ye see that, now? No sooner I lets it out than away it scuds!"

Under other circumstances this observation would have sounded commonplace; here it was significant. The fragrant spiral, after wavering an instant as if uncertain what course to take, broke and floated slowly towards the wall of *débris* which blocked the entrance.

"Wery good!" resumed the captain, when this became apparent; "an' what o' that? you naterally axes. Why, do ye mind me, lad, when smoke sheers off to lee'ard in that 'ere fashion, it sinnifies a drorin'; and a drorin', d'ye see, sinnifies a current o' atmospheric air; and—as the maintop-gallan's'l says when it sights the squall—blow me! if a current o' atmospheric air don't sinnify as this 'ere subterraneous ramification's got a venthole in it somewheres, d'ye see!"

"Why, as for that," said Don, "I noticed a draught drawing up the steps as soon as I set foot on them. The entrance seemed to act like a sort of flue; and, come to think of it, it couldn't do that, in spite of the heated air above, unless there was an inlet somewhere below, could it?"

"Ay, inlet's the wery nautical tarm I was a-tryin' to overhaul, lad," replied the captain complacently. "An'—shiver my binnacle!—for that inlet we runs. Legs we has, light we has!—so why not? I axes."

"More grope than run, I fancy," said Don, peering into the darkness of the tunnel. "But there's no help for it, I suppose; though Heaven only knows where or what it may lead to! The stores, of course, remain here for the present; they're safe enough, at any rate."

Seizing the lantern, he led off without further parley. Spottie—haunted in the dark by an ever-pursuing fear of spooks—made a close second; while the old sailor brought up the rear with Bosin on his shoulder. Here and there a lizard, alarmed by the hollow echo of their footsteps, or by the glare of the passing light, scurried across their path.

For a considerable distance the passage continued on the level, then dipped suddenly in a steep flight of steps. After this came other level bits, succeeded by other descents, the number of steps in each successive flight—or, rather, fall—increasing as they proceeded.

"Looks as if we were bound for the foot of the hill," remarked Don, pausing to allow the captain to overtake him.

"An' well I knows it, lad!" replied that worthy, as he accomplished the descent of that particular flight of steps with a sigh of relief like the blowing of a small whale. "Sleepin' in the open an' that, d'ye see, 's made my jints a bit stiff like—'specially the wooden one! Howsomedever, let's get on again—as the seaman says when the lubberly donkey rose by the starn an' hove him by the board."

On they accordingly went, and down, the level intervals growing less and less frequent, the seemingly interminable tiers of steps more precipitous. Even the captain, level-headed old sailor though he was, detected himself in the act of clutching at the wall, so suggestive of utter bottomlessness was the black chasm yawning ever at their feet. The very echoes hurried back to them as if fearful of venturing the abysmal depths. What it would have been to have penetrated the tunnel without a lantern Don dared not think.

And now the roof and walls contracted until they seemed to press with an insupportable weight upon their shoulders. The steps, too, at first equal in height and even of surface, became irregular and slippery. Ooze of a vivid prismatic green glistened on either hand; water gathered in pellucid, elongated drops overhead, shivered for an instant as if startled by the unwonted light, then glinted noiselessly down upon the dank, mould-carpeted steps, which no human foot apparently had pressed for ages. Suppose their advance, when they got a little lower, should be cut off by the water, as retreat was already cut off by the fallen wall!

A level footing at last! Twenty yards on through the darkness, and no steps. Had these come to an end? It almost seemed so.

Suddenly the captain stopped. On the rock floor a tiny pool shimmered like crystal in the lantern-light. He scooped up a little of the water in his broad palm and tasted it.

"Stave my water-butt, lad!" cried he, smacking his lips with immense gusto. "This 'ere aqueous fluid what's a-washin' round in the scuppers ain't no bilge-water, d'ye mind me! Reg'lar genewine old briny's what it is, an' well

L

I knows the taste on it! We're under the crik—blow me if we bain't!"

"Shouldn't wonder," said Don, consulting his watch. "It's now three o'clock; we've been on the grope just three-quarters of an hour. A jolly nice fix we'll be in if we reach daylight on the far side of the creek—with no means of crossing it, I mean. But wherever this mole-hole leads to, let's get to the end of it."

More steps, but this time ascending. The walls, too, became perceptibly drier, the narrow limits and musty air of the vaulted way less oppressive. With elastic steps and light hearts they pressed forward, assured that release was now close at hand.

It came sooner than they anticipated, for presently the tunnel veered sharply to the left, and as Don rounded the angle of wall a low, musical lapping of waves fell on his ears.

The captain was right in his conjecture; the passage had conducted them directly under the creek, and it was on that side of the ravine immediately adjacent to the Elephant Rock that they now emerged into the fresh night air.

Here the tunnel terminated in a platform of rock, escarped from the solid cliff, and draped by a curtain of vines similar to, though somewhat thinner than, that which concealed the hiding-place of the *Jolly Tar*. The platform itself lay wrapped in deepest shade, but through the interstices of the natural curtain overhanging it they could see the moonlight shimmering on the surface of the creek.

"Blow me, lad!" cried the captain, after peering about him for some seconds: "this 'ere cove as we're hove-to in orter lay purty nigh abreast o' the *Jolly Tar*, says you. Belay that, ye lubber!" making a dive after the monkey, who, with a shrill cry, had swung down from his shoulder and scuttled to the edge of the platform.

Don gripped the old sailor by the arm and forcibly held him back. "Hist!" he cried in suppressed, excited tones. "Did you hear that?"

A moment of strained silence; then, from the direction of the creek came a faint plashing sound, such as might have been produced by the regular dip of paddles. Releasing his hold on the captain's arm, Don crossed the rocky floor on tiptoe, parted the trailing vines with cautious hand, and took a rapid survey of the moonlit creek. Then he hastily seized the monkey and darted back to the captain's side.

"Canoes!" he whispered. "Two of them, packed with natives, and heading straight for us. Back into the passage! And, Spottie! douse that light."

CHAPTER XII.

RELATES HOW A WRONG ROAD LED TO THE RIGHT PLACE.

THEY had barely gained the shelter of the tunnel and extinguished the light, when the prows of the canoes grated against the rock, and a number of natives scrambled out upon the platform, jabbering loudly.

Would they remain there, or enter the tunnel where the little band of unarmed adventurers—for the captain had neglected to fetch a musket, and Don to load his pistols—lay concealed? It was a moment of breathless suspense. Then a torch was lighted, and the intruders, to the number of perhaps a score, filed off to the right and disappeared.

When the last echo of their footsteps had died away, the captain heaved a sigh of relief, and bade Spottie relight the lantern.

"Not that I be afear'd o' the warmints, d'ye mind me, lad," said he, as if in apology for the sigh; "only—spike my guns!—a couple o' brace o' fists 'ud be short rations to set under the noses o' sich a rampageous crew, d'ye see. Howsomedever, the way's clear at last, as the shark says when he'd swallied the sailor; so beat up to wind'ard a bit, till we diskiver whereaway the warmints's bound for."

"There's another passage, most likely," observed Don, holding the lantern aloft at arm's length as they left the tunnel behind and re-emerged upon the rock platform. "Ha! there it is, captain; yonder, in the far corner."

"Right ye are, lad," replied the captain with a chuckle. "We'll inwestigate into this 'ere subterraneous ramification, says you; so forge ahead, my hearty."

The entrance to the second tunnel was quickly gained, and into it, as nothing was either to be seen or heard of the natives, they "inwestigated" —to use the captain's phraseology—as far as a flight of steps which extended upwards for an unknown distance beyond the limits of the lantern's rays. Here the captain paused, and bending forward:

"Scrapers an' holystones, lad!" cried he with a chuckle; "the quarterdeck of a ship-o'-the-line itself ain't cleaner'n these 'ere steps. Native feet goin' aloft and a-comin' down continual, that's what's scraped 'em, says you; an' so I gets an idee. This 'ere subterraneous carawan as we've been an' diskivered is the tail o' the 'Elephant'!"

"The what, captain?" cried Don.

"Why, d'ye mind me, lad," the captain proceeded to explain, "when them lubberly landswabs as pilots elephants—which I means mahouts, d'ye see—when they wants to go aloft, so to say, how does they manage the business? I axes. They lays hold on the warmint's tail, says you, and up they goes over the starn. Wery good! This 'ere's a Elephant Rock as we're at the present moment inwestigatin' into, d'ye mind me, an' when betimes the lubberly crew as mans it is ordered aloft onto the animile's back, why, up these 'ere steps they goes. An' so I calls 'em the tail o' the 'Elephant'—an' why not? I axes."

Don gripped the old sailor's hand impulsively. "Hurrah! this discovery's worth a dozen hours' groping underground, captain!" he cried. "For if the natives can gain the Elephant Rock by following this passage, why can't we do the same?

Jack, old boy, if you're still alive—which you are, please God!—we'll find you yet!"

"Ay, at the risk of our wery lives, if need be!" responded the captain, in tones that lost none of their heartiness through being a bit husky. "An' the bag o' pearls, too, for the matter o' that, lad," he added; "for, d'ye see, as the old song says:

> We always be ready,
> Steady, lad, steady!
> We'll fight an' we'll conquer agin and agin!

Howsomedever, fightin' without wittles ain't to be thought of, no more'n without powder, says you; so 'bout ship an' bear away for the Ha'nted Pagolas!"

"Thank Heaven for the fire and that tumbledown wall!" ejaculated Don as they retraced their steps to the platform. "Chance has done for us what no planning—or fighting either, for the matter of that—could ever have done. We started on a wrong road, but, all the same, it has led us to the right place."

"Ay, lad, only chance bain't the right word for it, d'ye see. There's a Providence, lad, as sits up aloft," said the captain, lifting his cap reverently. "I bain't, so to say, a religious cove; but, storm or calm, them's the wery identical words as I always writes in my log. An', d'ye mind me, lad, 'tis the hand o' the Good Pilot as has guided us here to-night."

"I don't doubt it," replied Don gravely, "any more than I doubt that the same Good Pilot will guide us safely into port. Bearing that in mind, we have only to mature our plans and end the whole thing at a stroke. Here we are, and now for the creek," he concluded, crossing the platform and thrusting aside the pendent vines. "We'll borrow one of the canoes those niggers came in. Hullo, they're gone!"

"Some of the lubberly crew stopped aboard and rowed off agin, belike," observed the captain. "Blow me, if we shan't have to take to the water, as the sailors said when they'd swallied all the rum."

Don made no reply, but rapidly divesting himself of his coat and shoes, he slipped into the water before the old sailor well knew what he was about.

"I'm off for the canoe we hid in the jungle," he called back as he struck out for the other shore.

"Ay, ay, lad!" responded the captain; "an' here's to your speedy retarn, as the shark says when they hoisted the sailor into the ship's gig."

Swimming the creek was, after all, an insignificant feat for a sturdy-limbed young fellow like Don. The water was warm and refreshing, the distance far from great. A dozen vigorous strokes, and he was well within the deep shadow of the opposite cliff, for he deemed it prudent to avoid the moonlight, lest by any chance the natives who had removed the canoes should be in the vicinity.

Once, indeed, he fancied he actually heard a faint splashing in the water a short distance ahead. He floated for a moment, motionless and alert; but as the noise was not repeated, he swam on again. He had made scarce half-a-dozen strokes, however, when he suddenly felt himself gripped from below by the leg. His first thought was of sharks; his next, that he was in the clutches of a human foe, for a vice-like hand was at his throat.

CHAPTER XIII.

CAPTAIN MANGO "GOES ALOFT."

SELF-PRESERVATION is the first law of life, and no sooner did Don feel that iron grip compressing his throat, and dragging him down into the depths of the creek, than he struck out to such good purpose that the hold of his unknown assailant quickly relaxed. As he shot up to the surface he found himself confronted by the dripping head and shoulders of a native. A brief cessation of hostilities followed; each glared at the other defiantly, the native's tense breathing and watchful eye indicating that, though baffled for the moment by his opponent's prompt defensive measures, he was in no two minds about renewing the struggle.

Suddenly, by a lightning-like movement of the hand, he dashed a blinding jet of spray into Don's eyes, instantly followed up the advantage thus treacherously gained, grappled with him, and pinioned his arms tightly at his sides. Then, to his horror, Don felt his head thrust violently back, felt the fellow's hot, quick breath on his neck, and his teeth gnashing savagely at his throat.

Luckily for himself Don was no mean athlete, and knew how to use his fists to advantage when occasion demanded. Wrenching his arms free, he seized the native by the throat, and in spite of his eel-like slipperiness and desperate struggles, by an almost superhuman effort forced him slowly backwards until he had him at effective striking distance, when, suddenly loosing his hold, he let him have a tremendous "one-two" straight from the shoulder, that stretched the native senseless and bleeding on the water.

"You would have it!" he panted, surveying the native's sinewy proportions with grim satisfaction. "Next time you won't wait to be knocked out, I reckon. But 'twon't do to let you drown, though you richly deserve it; so come along, you black cub!"

Seizing the black by the convenient tuft of hair at the back of his bullet-head, he towed him to the strip of beach, and there hauled him out upon the sand, directly into a patch of moonlight, as it happened, that came slanting down through a rift in the canopy of palm-leaves overhead. Something in the appearance of the upturned features caused him to drop on his knees at the native's side.

"Hullo!" he cried, peering into the fellow's face, "Jack's lascar, as I'm alive! By Jove, you are a prize! We'll keep you with us longer than we did last time, my friend. Ha, ha! won't the captain chuckle, though!"

With his belt he proceeded to strap the lascar's hands securely behind his back; but when it came to fastening his legs, a difficulty cropped up. That is to say, the strap could not be used for both, and he had no substitute. Fortunately the lascar wore about his loins the regulation length of strong country cotton—his only covering—and this Don was in the act of removing when a knife fell out of its folds.

"Lucky thing I didn't run against you in the water," he soliloquised, picking the weapon up. "Why, it's the very knife the lascar shot at Jack from the schooner's deck; the one he let the fellow have back for sending the boathook through the cutter's side; and that we afterwards found lying in the *ballam* here. And yet Jack certainly had it on him when those niggers carried him off. So, old chap," apostrophising the insensible owner of the much-bandied knife, "so you had a hand in kidnapping him too, had you? All the more reason for caring for you now that we've got you."

Following up this idea, he knotted the cloth tightly about the lascar's legs, dragged him well up the beach, and went in search of the canoe. This, fortunately, had not been molested in their absence; in a few minutes he had it in the water. Then, seizing the paddle, he propelled the light skiff swiftly in the direction of the rock platform, where he found the old sailor stumping his beat in a terrible state of uneasiness over his prolonged absence.

"Spike my guns, lad!" cried he, bearing down upon the young man with outstretched hand and a smile as broad as the cutter's mainsail, "they warmints's been an' done for Master Don this hitch, I says to myself when the half-hour fails to bring ye. An' what manner o' mishap's kept ye broached-to all this while? I axes."

"Fact is, captain, I was attacked by the enemy. Came within an ace of being captured, too. But, as good luck would have it, I managed to get in a thundering broadside, boarded the enemy—there was only one, luckily—spiked his guns, and towed him ashore, where he's waiting to pay his respects to you now. But get in and see for yourself what a valuable prize I've taken."

The captain got in with all despatch, and, as soon as the canoe touched the opposite beach, got out again without delay, so eager was he to inspect the captive. As it was now daylight, he recognised the fellow the moment he set eyes on him. His delight knew no bounds. Round and round the luckless lascar he stumped, chuckling as he always did when he was pleased, and every now and then prodding him in the ribs with his wooden leg, as if to reassure himself that he laboured under no delusion.

"Sharks an' sea-sarpents, lad!" he roared, when quite satisfied as to the lascar's identity, "we'll keep the warmint fast in the bilboes a while, says you; for, d'ye mind me, he's old Salambo's right-hand man, is this lubber, as comes an' goes at his beck an' call, an' executes the orders as he gives. So in the bilboes he remains; why not? I axes."

"My idea precisely, captain. He can't be up to any of his little games so long as he has a good stout strap to hug him; and, what's more, he'll have a capital chance to recover from that nasty slash Jack gave him the other night. By the way, I've often wondered, do you know, how he managed to pull through that affair so easily. Suppose we turn him over and have a look at his shoulder?"

No sooner said than done, notwithstanding the captive's snarling protests; but, to their great amazement, his shoulder showed neither wound nor scar.

"Well, this beats me!" exclaimed Don incredulously.

"An' is this the wery identical swab, an' no mistake? I axes," demanded the captain.

"Mistake? None whatever, unless Jack was mistaken in the fellow the other day, which isn't at all likely. Besides, I've seen him twice before myself; once in the temple, and again on the sands here. I'd know that hang-dog look of his among a thousand. Then there's Spottie; he saw him as well. Stop! let's see what Spottie makes of this."

Spottie was summoned, and, without being informed of the point in dispute, unhesitatingly identified the captive as the lascar.

"Then," said Don, "Jack must have supposed he stabbed the fellow when he didn't; that's the most I can make of it."

"Belay there!" objected the captain. "What about the blood in the canoe and on the knife when arterwards found? I axes."

"There you have me. This fellow's the lascar fast enough; but how he's the lascar and yet doesn't show the wound Jack gave him, I know no more than the man in the moon. Ugh! what a greasy beast he is! I'd better take the strap up another hole to make sure of him."

So, for a time, the puzzling question of the lascar's identity dropped.

No food being procurable here, they decided to push on to the Haunted Pagodas ere the sun became too hot, and there endeavour to clear a passage to the immured stores. Accordingly, when the canoe had been dragged back to its former place of concealment, they set out, Don taking charge of the lascar, who, clad in Spottie's upper-cloth, and having his legs only at liberty, led as quietly as a lamb.

Two-thirds of the way up they came upon that portion of the hill which had been ravaged by the fire. For the most part this had now burnt itself out, leaving the summit of the elevation one vast bed of ghastly gray ashes, with here and there a smouldering stump or cluster of bamboo stems still smoking.

At the Haunted Pagodas two surprises awaited them. The first of these was no other than Puggles himself, alive and lachrymose. On the floor of the otherwise empty "fo'csle" he sat, blubbering dolefully. Comical indeed was the spectacle he presented, with his woebegone face thickly begrimed with a mixture of ashes and tears —a sort of fortuitous whitewash, relieved in the funniest fashion by the black skin showing in patches through its lighter veneer, and by the double line of vivid red, stretching half-way from ear to ear, that marked the generous expanse of his mouth.

The explanation of his sudden disappearance proved simple enough. He had stumbled in the very act of following his master past the swiftly-advancing fire, and crawling back on hands and knees to a place of safety, had there passed the night alone in the jungle. On reaching the encampment and finding it deserted, he jumped to the conclusion that the fire had, as he put it, "done eat sahibs up," stores and all. Hence his tearful condition on their return.

The second surprise was one of an equally pleasing nature, since it concerned the stores. The mass of *débris* which blocked the tunnel's mouth had subsided to such an extent in cooling as to admit of their reaching the imprisoned stores with but little difficulty.

" All the same, captain," remarked Don, when presently they began a vigorous attack on the provisions, " I'm jolly glad our fear of being buried alive drove us to the far end of the hole. We've got the key to the Elephant Rock, and, what's more, we've got a grip on old Salambo's right hand," nodding towards the lascar, who was again bound hand and foot, " that's safe to stand us in good stead when it comes to the final tussle for Jack and the pearls."

" Right ye are, lad," said the captain in tones as hearty as his appetite; "an', blow me!—as the fog-horn says to the donkey-ingin—arter we snatches a wink o' sleep, d'ye mind me, we'll lay our heads together a bit an' detarmine on the best course to be steered."

On the stone floor of the "fo'csle" the blacks were already sleeping the sleep of repletion; and, their meal finished, Don and the captain lost no time in following their example—for thirty-six hours of almost unremitting exertion and danger had told heavily upon their powers of endurance. Dead tired as they were, they gave little heed to the lascar beyond assuring themselves by a hasty glance that his bonds were secure. To all appearance he was wrapped in profound slumber.

The sun was at the zenith when they stretched themselves upon the flags of the "fo'csle"; slowly it burnt its way downward to the western horizon, and still they slept. Don was the first to stir. He raised himself upon his elbow with a yawn, rubbed his eyes, gazed about him in momentary bewilderment. Twilight had already crept out of the ravine and invaded the ghostly, fire-scathed ruins. This was the first thing he noticed. Then the recollection of the events of the past day and night rushed upon him, and he turned abruptly, with a sudden vague sense of dread, to the spot where the lascar lay.

Lay? No; that place was empty!

He could scarcely believe the evidence of his senses. Had the fellow somehow managed to shift his position, and roll out of sight behind one of the numerous blocks of stone that lay about? Or had he——

With a cry of alarm he threw himself upon an object that lay where the lascar had lain. It was the leathern belt with which he had bound the fellow's arms. The tongue of the buckle was broken. He recollected now, and almost cursed his folly for not recollecting before, that the buckle had long been weak. Too late! The lascar had escaped!

Dashing the traitorous belt upon the stones, he hurried to where the old sailor lay asleep, with Bosin curled up by his side, and shook him roughly by the shoulder. He was in no gentle mood just then.

"Captain! Captain! Wake up! The lascar's off!"

No response. No movement. Only the monkey awoke suddenly and fell to whimpering.

The captain lay at full length upon his back, his bronzed hands clasped upon his broad chest, his blue sailor's cap drawn well over his eyes. Something in the pose of the figure at his feet, in its stillness—something, too, in the plaintive half-human wail the monkey uttered at the moment—struck a sudden chill to Don's heart. He dropped upon his knees, lifted the cap, peered into the upturned face. It was distorted, purple. He started back with a fearful cry :

"Not dead! Oh, my God, not dead!"

CHAPTER XIV.

SHROUDED IN A HAMMOCK.

That was a fearful moment for Don. The quest of the golden pearl, entered upon with all the love of adventure and sanguine hope natural to young hearts, began to wear a serious aspect indeed. Even had Jack been there to share the heartbreak of it, this sudden, numbing blow would still have been terribly hard to bear. But Jack was gone—whither, Heaven alone knew—and the captain was dead.

Ay, the "Providence that sits up aloft" had at last looked out a snug berth for the old sailor, and shipped him for the Eternal Voyage. Kneeling by his side in the solemn twilight, with aching heart Don recalled all his quaint ways and quainter sayings, his large-hearted generosity, his rollicking good-nature, his rough but ever-ready sympathy—and sealed the kindly eyes with such tears as are wrung from us but once or twice in a lifetime, and recalled with sadness often, with shame never.

But for him the captain would never have undertaken this disastrous venture. This was the bitterest, the sorest thought of all.

At last Bosin's low wailing broke in upon his sad reverie. Well-nigh human did the monkey seem, as with tender, lingering touch he caressed his master's face, and sought to rouse him from this strange sleep of which he felt but could not understand the awful meaning. Then, failing to win from the dumb lips the response he craved, he turned his eyes upon his master's friend with a look of pathetic appeal fairly heartbreaking in its mute intensity.

No sooner did he succeed in attracting Don's attention, however, than his manner underwent a complete change. The plaintive wail became a hiss, the puny, lithe hands tore frantically at something that showed like a thin, dark streak about the dead man's neck. What with the waning light and the shock of finding the captain dead, Don had not noticed this streak before. He looked at it closely now, and as he looked a horrified intelligence leapt into his face. The dark streak was a cord: the captain had been strangled !

Oh, the horror of that discovery! Hitherto he had suspected no foul play, no connection of any kind, indeed, between the captain's death and the lascar's escape; for had he not taken the precaution to disarm the native? But now he remembered seeing that cord about the fellow's middle. He had thought it harmless. Harmless! Ah, how different was the mute witness borne by the old sailor's lifeless form! In the lascar's hands the cord had proved an instrument of death as swift and sure as any knife.

But why had the captain been singled out as the victim? Was the lascar merely bent on wreaking vengeance on those who had injured him? Or was he a tool in other and invisible hands?

Feverishly he asked himself these questions as he removed the fatal cord, and composed the distorted features into a semblance of what they had been in life; asked, but could not answer them. Only, back of the whole terrible business, he seemed to see the cunning, unscrupulous shark-charmer, bent on retaining the pearls at any cost, fanning the lascar's hatred into fiercer flame, guiding his ready hand in its work of death.

Could he, alone and all but unaided, cope with the cunning of this enemy who, while himself unseen, made his devilish power felt at every turn? The responsibility thrown upon his shoulders by the captain's murder involved other and weightier issues than the mere recovery of a few thousand pounds' worth of stolen pearls. Jack must be rescued, if indeed he was still alive; while, if he too was dead, his and the captain's murderers must be brought to justice. This was the task before him; no light one for a youth of eighteen, with only a brace of timid native servants at his back. Yet he addressed himself to it with all the passionate determination born of his love for the chum and his grief for the friend who had stood by him "through thick and thin." There was no hesitation, no wavering. "Do or die!" It was come to that now.

The captain's burial must be his first consideration; for Don had lived long enough in the East to know how remorseless is the climate in its treatment of the dead. Morning at the latest must snatch the old sailor's familiar form for ever from his sight.

A tarpaulin lay in the "fo'csle," and with this he determined to hide the lascar's dread handiwork from view before waking the blacks, who still slept. While he was disposing this appropriate pall above the corpse, the captain's jacket fell open, and in an inside pocket he caught sight of a small volume.

"Perhaps he has papers about him that ought to be preserved," thought Don. "I'll have a look."

Drawing the volume from its resting-place with reverent touch, he found it to be a copy of the Book of Common Prayer, sadly worn and battered, like its owner, by long service. Here and there a leaf was turned down, or a passage marked by the dent of a heavy thumb-nail—the sailor's pencil. But what arrested his attention were these words, written on the yellow fly-leaf in a bold, irregular hand, and in ink so faded as to make it evident that many years had elapsed since they were penned:

"To all and sundry as sights these lines, whensomedever it may please the Good Skipper to tow this 'ere old hulk safe into port, widelicit. If so be as I'm spared to go aloft when on the high-seas, wery good! the loan of a hammock and a bit o' ballast is all I axes. But if so be as I'm ewentually stranded on shore, why then, d'ye mind me, whosomedever ye be as sights these 'ere lines, I ain't to be battened down like a lubberly landsman, d'ye see, but warped off-shore an' shipped for the Eternal V'yage as a true seaman had ought to be. And may God have mercy on my soul.—Amen. The last Log and Testament of me,

"(Signed) JOHN MANGO, A. B."

The faded characters grew blurred and misty before Don's eyes as he scanned them. Closing the book, he grasped the captain's cold hand impulsively, and in tones choked with emotion, cried :

"You shall have your wish, dear old friend! We'll warp you off-shore and ship you for the Eternal Voyage in a way befitting the true seaman that you are."

And the mute lips seemed to smile back their approval, as though they would say :

"Ay, ay, why not, I axes? An' cheer up, my hearty, for, d'ye mind me, lad, pipin' your eye won't stop the leak when the ship's a-sinkin'."

What boots it to linger over the noisy, but none the less genuine grief, of the faithful Spottie when he learned the sad truth ? Nor is it necessary to describe at length the sad preparations for consigning the dead captain to his long home beneath the waves that had been his home so long in life. Suffice it to say that without loss of time a rude bier was constructed on which to convey the remains to the beach, and that while this was preparing there occurred an event so remarkable, and withal of so important a bearing upon the future of the quest, as to merit something more than mere passing mention.

It happened while the three were in the jungle cutting materials for the litter, and it concerned the fatal cord.

" Until the lascar's paid out, I'll keep this as a reminder of what I owe him," Don had said grimly, just before starting; and taking the lascar's knife from his belt he stuck it into a crevice in the "fo'csle" wall, and hung the snake-like cord upon it.

Spottie and Puggles being too timid to leave with the dead, or to send alone into the jungle in quest of materials for the bier—for was it not at nightfall that shadowy spooks walked abroad?— Don was forced to bear them company. There was no help for it; the captain's body must be left unguarded in their absence—except, indeed, for such watch-care as puny Bosin was able to give it.

Up to the moment of their setting out the monkey had not for a single instant left his master's side. This fact served to render all the more extraordinary the discovery they made on their return—namely, that the monkey had quitted his post. What could have induced him to abandon his master at such a moment was a mystery.

And the mystery deepened when Don, wanting the knife, sought it in the "fo'csle," for, to his astonishment, neither knife nor cord was to be found.

"Dey spooks done steal um, sar," cried Spottie, with chattering teeth.

"Huh," objected Puggles, between whom and Spottie there had grown up a sharp rivalry during their brief acquaintance, "why they no steal dead sahib? I axes." Then to his master: "Lascar maybe done come back, sahib."

This suggestion certainly smacked more of plausibility than that offered by Spottie, since it not only accounted for the disappearance of the cord and knife, but of Bosin as well. Was it too much to believe that the faithful creature's hatred, instinctively awakened by the lascar's stealthy return, had outweighed affection for his dead master and impelled him to abandon the one that he might track the other? Remembering the intelligence exhibited by the monkey in the past, Don at least was satisfied that this explanation was the true one.

By midnight all was in readiness, and with heavy hearts they took up their dead and began the toilsome descent to the creek. This reached, the *Jolly Tar* was drawn from her place of concealment, and the captain's body lashed in a tarpaulin. Then, with white wings spread, the cutter bore silently away from the creek's mouth in quest of a last resting-place for the master whose behest she was never again to obey.

"This will do," said Don, when a half-hour's run had put them well off-shore. "Take the tiller, Pug, and keep her head to the wind for a little."

With bowed head he opened the well-worn Prayer Book, and, while the waves chanted a solemn funeral dirge, read in hushed tones the office for the burial of the dead at sea. A pause, a tear glinting in the moonlight, a splash—and just as the morning star flashed out like a beacon above the eastern sea-rim, the old sailor began the Eternal Voyage.

"And now," said Don, as he brought the cutter's head round in the direction of the creek; "now for the last tussle and justice for the dead. Let me only come face to face once more with that murderous lascar or his master, and no false notions of mercy shall stay my hand—so help me Heaven!"

And surely not Heaven itself could deem that vow unrighteous.

CHAPTER XV.

THE CROCODILE PIT.

The last melancholy duty to the captain discharged, Don threw himself heart and fist—as Jack would have said—into the work cut out for him; and by the time the *Jolly Tar* was again rubbing her nose against the inner wall of the grotto, he had decided to abandon the Haunted Pagodas and to make this secluded spot—next door to the back entrance of the Elephant Rock—his base of operations.

"Up to now it's been all take and no give," he said to himself; "but now we've got to act, and act like a steel trap, sharp and sure. What is it the old school motto says?—'bis dat qui cito dat,' 'a quick blow's as good as two any day.' The old Roman who strung that together knew what he was talking about, anyhow, and I'll put his old saw to the test before another sun sets."

In the letter of which Bosin had been the bearer Jack had said—"They take me to the Elephant Rock to-night." Twice since then had night come and gone; and if his chum had not perished in the village holocaust, in the Elephant Rock he was probably to be found. Hurrah for the finding!

The muskets were still at the "fo'csle," for that sad midnight descent of the hill had left their hands too full for weapons. Besides, none were needed then. They were needed now, however, so there was nothing for it but to climb the hill after them. This, and the time necessarily consumed in snatching a hasty meal, delayed the start by a good two hours.

At length all was ready, and tumbling into the canoe they pushed off. To stick to the literal truth, Spottie did the tumbling. In spite of all his efforts to assume a dignity of carriage in keeping with his weapons and the occasion, the cutlass at Spottie's belt would persist in getting at cross-purposes with his long, thin legs, and so throw him, physically speaking, off his balance. Once seated in the canoe, however, with the point of the cutlass in dangerous proximity to Puggles's back, and the old flint-lock so disposed upon his knees as to hit Don to a dead certainty if by any mischance it went off, Spottie looked exceedingly fierce—in fact, an out-and-out swashbuckler.

Not so Puggles. No weapons could make him look other than what nature had made him—a happy-go-lucky, fun-and-food loving, sunny-faced lump of oily blackness. The extra broad grin that tugged at the far corners of his expansive mouth proclaimed him at peace with all the world—especially with that important section of it bounded by his swelling waistband—and gave the lie direct to his warlike equipment.

Of crossing the creek Don made short work, and soon they stood upon the rock platform, where, but little more than twenty-four hours before, the landing and sudden disappearance of the native crew had put them in possession of the key which was now, if fortune favoured them, to unlock the secret of Jack's fate, and, haply, the door of his prison-house.

Yonder on the right—for the spot was light enough by day, despite its curtain of vegetation—could be seen the black mouth of the tunnel running under the creek, and so to the summit of Haunted Pagoda Hill; here, on the left, that by which the natives had taken their departure. It was with this that Don's business lay now; and as he led the way into it he recalled with a sorrowful smile that quaint fancy of the captain's which made this approach to the Rock "the tail o' the Elephant." And here was the very spot where he had uttered the words. He almost fancied he could see the old sailor standing there still, his wooden leg thrust well forward, his cap well back, and Bosin perched contentedly upon his broad shoulder. Alas for fancy!

But what was this that came leaping down the dim vista of steps? No creature of fancy surely, but actual flesh and blood. Only flesh and blood in the form of a monkey, it is true, but what mattered that, since the monkey was none other than Bosin himself?

A jubilant shout from Puggles greeted his appearance—a shout which Don, fearful of discovery, immediately checked—while Spottie made as if to catch the returned truant. But the impish Bosin would have none of him; eluding the grasp of the black, he sprang upon Don's shoulder. Only then did Don observe that the monkey was not empty-handed. He carried something hugged tightly against his breast.

Like all his tribe, Bosin had a pretty *penchant*

for annexing any chance article that happened to take his fancy, without regard to ordinary rights of property.

"Prigging again, eh?" said Don, as he gently disengaged the monkey's booty from his grasp. "What have you got this time?"

To his astonishment he saw that he held in his hands the lascar's cord, and—surely he was not mistaken?—the fellow to that half of Jack's handkerchief in which his letter had been wrapped up when despatched from the village per monkey post.

Bosin's mysterious disappearance, then, was explained. In quitting his dead master's side so unaccountably he had had a purpose in view—a monkeyish, unreasoning purpose, doubtless, but none the less a purpose—which was none other than to track the lascar to his lair and regain possession of the cord. Not that he knew in the least the value to Don of the yard of twisted hemp, or the significance of the scrap of crumpled, bloodstained cambric he was at such pains to filch. With only blind instinct for his guide, he had been guided better than he knew; for while the cord proved the Elephant Rock to be the hiding-place of the lascar, the handkerchief proved, or seemed to prove, that Jack was still alive and that the lascar's hiding-place was his prison.

Don's heart leapt at the discovery.

Perhaps Jack, unable for some reason to scribble even so much as a word, had entrusted the handkerchief to the monkey's care, knowing that the sight of it would assure his chum of his safety, if it did no more. Or perhaps Bosin had carried it off while Jack slept?

A thousand conjectures flashed through Don's brain, but he thrust them hastily aside, since mere conjecture could not release his chum; and calling to the blacks to follow, he sprang up the steps with a lighter heart. The monkey swung himself down from his perch and took the lead, as if instinctively divining the object of their quest; chattering gleefully when the trio pressed close upon his heels — impatiently when they lagged behind.

The steps surmounted, they discovered an offshoot from the main tunnel, from which point of division the latter dwindled straight away into a mere dot of light in the distance. In the main tunnel itself the light was faint enough; but as they advanced it increased in brilliancy till presently — the distance being actually much less than the unbroken perspective of chiselled rock made it appear—they emerged suddenly into the broad light of day, streaming down through an oblong cleft or gash cut deep into the solid heart of the Rock.

The light itself was more welcome than what it revealed.

Directly across their path, at their very feet indeed, extended a yawning chasm, of depth unknown—but, as the first glance served to show, of such breadth as to effectually bar their further progress.

CHAPTER XVI.

DON SETS A DEATH-TRAP FOR THE LASCAR.

To be sure, skirting the end wall on the extreme left was a ledge along which the agile monkey made his way to the opposite side of the pit with little or no difficulty; but, as for following him, by that road at least, why, the thing was an utter impossibility. The ledge was a mere thread. Scarce a handbreadth of rock lay between the smooth-cut upper wall and the perpendicular face of the pit.

"Blow me!" muttered Don, unconsciously echoing the phrase he had so often heard on the captain's lips, "if this ain't the purtiest go as ever I see!" Which assertion was purely figurative; for as he was only too well aware it was "no go" at all, so far as the pit was concerned.

Peering over the brink of the chasm he found it to be partially filled with water, between which and the spot where he stood intervened perhaps thirty feet of sheer wall. An uninviting pool it looked, lying as green and putrescent within its sunken basin as if the bones of unnumbered dead men were rotting in its depths. The very sunshine that fell in a great golden blotch upon its surface seemed to shrink from its foul touch.

But what struck Don as the strangest feature of this noisome pool was the constant agitation of its waters. To what was it due? What were those black, glistening objects floating here and there upon its surface? And those others, ranged along the half-submerged ledge on the far side? A small fragment of stone chanced to lie near him. He picked it up and aimed it at one of these curious objects. To his astonishment the black mass slowly shifted its position and plunged with a wallowing splash into the pool. Puggles, who had been looking on with mouth agape, raised a shout.

"Him corkadile, sa'b! Me sometimes bery often seeing um in riber. Him plenty appetite got!"

"Ugh, the monsters!" muttered his master, watching with a sort of horrible fascination the movements of the hulking reptiles, which lifted their ugly, square snouts towards him as if scenting prey. "Here's a pretty kettle of fish! Crossing this hole is bound to be a tough job at the best—but, as if that wasn't enough, these brutes must turn up and add danger to difficulty. Plenty appetite? I should think so, indeed, in such a hole as this! However, crocodile or no crocodile, it's got to be crossed."

Until now he had rather wondered, to tell the truth, why it was that not a single native had crossed their path. He had expected to find the passage guarded. The pit, not to say the crocodiles, shed a flood of light—not very cheering light, he was forced to admit—upon this point. No doubt the natives considered themselves in little danger from intrusion, so long as they were guarded by a dozen feet of sheer pit, with a dozen brace or so of healthy crocodiles at the bottom of it.

And probably they were right so far as concerned intruders of their own colour and pluck; but Don was made of sturdier stuff than native clay. Beyond the crocodile pit lay his chum, a prisoner. Cross it he must, and would. Therefore, to borrow the expressive phrase of an American humorist, he "rose to the emergency and caved the emergency's head in."

Was the pit too wide to leap? Spanning it

with his eye, he estimated its width at a dozen feet; certainly not less. A tremendous leap that, and fraught with fearful risk. And even should he be able to take it, what of Spottie and Puggles? They would never dare face it. And what, too, of the muskets and cutlasses?

Suddenly he descried, just where the continuation of the tunnel pierced the wall on the far side of the pit, an object that inspired him with fresh hope and determination. True, it was nothing more than a plank, but once that plank was in his hands, he could, perhaps, bridge the pit.

A dozen feet at the very least! Could he clear it? To jump short of the opposite ledge, to reach it, even, and then slip, meant certain and horrible death at the jaws of the crocodiles. Should he venture? Jack had ventured much for him. He slipped off his shoes—his stockinged feet would afford a surer foothold—and quietly bade the blacks stand aside. Sauntering carelessly into the tunnel —that by which they had approached the pit—a distance of forty paces or so, he turned, drew a deep breath, threw all his lithe strength into the short run, his whole soul into the leap, and—— Would he clear it?

No—yes! A horrified shriek from the blacks,

and he was over, the pit a scant handbreadth behind him.

Dragging the plank from its place of partial concealment, he was delighted to find a short piece of rope attached to it. Good; it would facilitate the bridging of the chasm. Standing on the brink, he coiled the rope—not without a misgiving that it was too short for his purpose—and, calling to Spottie to catch the end, threw it out over the pit sailor-fashion. It fell short.

"Stop!" cried he. "This will make it right;" and drawing the lascar's cord from his pocket, he knotted it to the rope. This time Spottie succeeded in grasping the end; and so, with the aid of the lascar's cord, the plank was drawn across. Its length was such that it bridged the pit from wall to wall, with a foot of spring-way to spare at either end.

At the time Don thought nothing of this apparently trivial incident; yet, had he but known it, with that cord he had laid a death-trap for the captain's murderer.

CHAPTER XVII.

THE BLAST OF A CONCH-SHELL.

THE rest was easy. In five minutes the blacks had crawled across, with many fearful glances at the upturned snouts of the huge reptiles below; and Don, treading the springy length of plank with sure foot, had transferred muskets and cutlasses to what he mentally termed "Jack's side" of the chasm. They were now ready for a fresh start.

All this time Bosin had watched their movements with an expression of mingled shrewdness and approval in his restless eyes that seemed to say: "Ha! the very thing I'd do myself were I in the fix you're in." Again he took the lead, like one who had travelled the road before, and was quite satisfied in his own mind that he knew all its little ins and outs.

His knowledge of the way became more apparent still when, after penetrating the heart of the rock for some distance, the tunnel split into three distinct branches. This point Don hesitated to pass; but not so Bosin. Without a pause he took the passage to the right, glancing back as if to assure himself that he was followed. Off this gallery others opened, until it became evident that, as the captain had once affirmed, the rock was honeycombed "from maindeck to keelson." But for the monkey's guidance Don must have found himself utterly at a loss amid so perplexing a labyrinth. As it was, he pressed forward with confidence.

Danger of discovery, owing to the multiplicity of passages, now increased momentarily. Any of these ghostly corridors might afford concealment to an enemy who, warned of danger by the muffled echo of approaching steps, might steal away, silently and unobserved, and so raise the alarm. Though still in his stocking feet, Don instinctively found himself treading on tip-toe, while the bare-footed blacks—who were even less inclined for a brush with the enemy than he— purposely did the same. Even then their movements, well-nigh noiseless though they were, caused commotion amongst the bats that clung in patches of living fungi to the vaulted roof, and sent them wheeling hither and thither in swift, startled flight.

To succeed in finding his chum, and to liberate him ere discovery came, was almost more than Don dared hope for. For come it must, sooner or later. Only, once Jack was by his side, he cared little how soon or in what manner it came. True, the natives possessed the seeming advantage of overwhelming numbers; but in these rock corridors the nozzle of a single musket was better than a hundred men.

To do him justice, he had thrust the pearls entirely out of his thoughts in his eagerness to set Jack at liberty. "Time enough to think about the pearls afterwards," he said to himself —forgetting that "afterwards" was at the best but a blind alley, full of unknown pitfalls.

They were now well into the heart of the Elephant Rock, where any moment might bring them face to face with Jack or his captors, or both.

At this point the monkey, who was some yards in advance, suddenly stopped and uttered a peculiar hissing sound. Once before—when, on the rock platform, Bosin had given warning of the approach of the canoes—had Don heard that hiss. There was no mistaking its significance. He motioned to the blacks to halt, and with stealthy tread crept forward alone.

Just ahead a sharp bend in the passage limited his view to a few yards of indifferently lighted wall. Hugging the inner side of this bend, he presently gained the jutting shoulder of rock which formed the dividing line between the vista of gallery behind and that ahead, and from this point of vantage peered cautiously round the projection in search of the cause of Bosin's alarm.

This was not far to seek. Immediately beyond the bend the passage expanded into a sort of vestibule, communicating, by means of a lofty portal, with a spacious, well-lighted chamber. It was not this discovery, however, that riveted his gaze, but a dusky figure crouched on the floor of the vestibule—the figure of a native, reclining on a mat, with his back to the spot where Don stood. By his side lay a sword of curious workmanship, and a huge conch-shell, the pearly pink of its inner surface contrasting strangely with the native's coffee-coloured skin. The weapon and the shell told their own tale: the native was doing "sentry-go."

Over what or whom? With swift glance Don scanned every nook and corner of the vestibule, and as much of the interior chamber as lay within range of his vision. So far as he could see both were empty, barring only the dusky sentinel. Then he fancied he heard the faint clanking of a chain, though from what direction the sound proceeded it was impossible to determine. Listening with bated breath, he heard it again, and now it seemed to come from the larger chamber. His pulses thrilled, and a determined light shone in his eyes as he turned them once more upon the sentinel.

"I'll jolly soon fix you, old chap," he said to himself; and noiselessly clubbing the musket he carried, he prepared to advance.

But for the monkey's vigilance he must have come upon the recumbent guard without the slightest warning, for not more than ten paces separated the shoulder of rock—Don's post of observation—from the mat on which the native reclined.

To fire upon him was out of the question, since that would fulfil the very purpose for which he, with his conch-shell trumpet, was stationed there —namely, to send a thousand wild echoes hurtling through chamber and galleries, and so apprise his comrades of impending danger. Moreover, Don had a wholesome horror of bloodshed, which at most times effectually held his trigger finger in check.

A swift, sure blow—that would be the best means of keeping the native's lips from the nozzle of his conch-trumpet. A blow—ay, there was the rub! For, though the native's back was towards him, the space by which they two were divided must be crossed; and these walls, dumb as they looked, had hidden tongues, which would echo and re-echo the faintest sound. Could he, then, get near enough to strike?

Inch by inch he crept towards the unconscious sentinel, slowly raising the butt of the musket as he advanced. So intense was the suspense of those few brief moments that he hardly breathed. It seemed as if the very beating of his heart must reach the native's ears. Inch by inch, foot by foot, until——

The native turned his head; but before he could spring to his feet, or even utter a cry, the musket crashed upon his shaven pate, and he rolled over on his side without a sound.

Don did not stop to ascertain the extent of his injuries. Neither did he summon the blacks. Again the clanking of chains rang in his ears, and at a bound he crossed the threshold of the larger

DON AND THE SENTINEL.

chamber. An unkempt human figure started up in the far corner.

"Jack!"

"And is it really you, old fellow?" cried Jack joyfully. "Give us your hand; and how did you find your way here, I want to know?"

"You have Bosin to thank for that," replied Don, returning his chum's grip with interest. "When I saw your handkerchief——"

"Ah, the monkey stole it, then! I missed it, don't you know, but never imagined that Bosin took it, though he paid me a visit early this morning. Well, he did me a good turn that time, anyhow."

"And a better one when he led us back here. But," continued Don in hurried, suppressed tones, "don't let us waste time palavering, Jack. There's not a moment to lose. I've done for old conchy yonder—knocked him on the head—but the rest may swoop down on us any minute. Say, how are you tethered?"

"Leg," said Jack laconically, rattling a chain which secured him to the wall. "Stop!"—as Don unslung his cutlass with the intention of hacking at the links—"I'll show you a trick worth two of that. You see that ring-bolt the chain's fastened to? Well, it's set in lead—not very securely as it happens—and I've managed to work it so loose that I fancy a good hard tug ought to bring it away. Meant to make off on my own account, you see, if you hadn't turned up, old fellow. But lay hold and let's have a pull for it, anyhow."

"Quick, then!" said Don. "I thought I heard footsteps."

Throwing their combined weight upon the chain, they pulled for dear life. The ring-bolt yielded little by little, and presently came away from its setting bodily, like an ancient tooth, and Jack was free. The chain, it is true, was still attached to his leg; but as it encircled only one ankle, this did not so much matter.

"Don't let it rattle," said Don breathlessly, "I'm positive I heard footsteps. And here, take this," thrusting the cutlass into Jack's disengaged hand. "Now, come on!"

Barely had he uttered the words when a hollow, prolonged blast, like that of a gigantic trumpet with a cold in its throat, filled the chamber with deafening clamour. And as the echoes leapt from wall to wall, and buffeted each other into silence, another sound succeeded them, faint and far away, but swelling momentarily into ominous loudness and nearness.

Don clutched his companion's arm.

"The fellow I knocked on the head—he's come

to!" he said thickly. "That was the blast of his conch; and this"—pausing with uplifted hand and bated breath until that other sound broke clearly on their ears—"this is the tread of heaven only knows how many native feet. Jack, we're discovered!"

CHAPTER XVIII.

BETWEEN LIFE AND DEATH.

Four galleries centred on the rock-chamber, and the confused, tumultuous rush of feet which followed the blast of the conch-shell like an ominous echo, proceeded from that particular gallery opposite the vestibule.

"Seems to be a rare lot of them; but we needn't stop to reckon 'em up," said Jack, with a constrained laugh. "Lead the way, old fellow."

Into the smaller chamber they dashed, to find the exit blocked by the sentinel with sword drawn. Rapidly reversing his musket, Don bore down upon him—he, to do him justice, standing his ground bravely—and with the butt-end of the weapon dealt the nigger a blow in the stomach that doubled him up like a broken bulrush.

"Where are the others?" cried Jack, as they rounded the shoulder of rock separating the antechamber from the passage. "You never came alone!"

"No; I left them just here—told them to wait," said Don, peering about in search of the blacks. "They must have gone back; thought they'd save their skins while they could, I suppose, the chicken-hearted beggars! Ha, here's Bosin, at any rate."

Swinging the monkey upon his shoulder, he set off at a run down the passage, Jack following as close as the weight of the chain would allow him to do. They had proceeded only a short distance when a faint, sepulchral shout brought them to a stand. The sound seemed to proceed from a gallery on their immediate right. The way out did not lie in that direction.

"That's Pug's wheeze," said Don. "They've taken the wrong turning;" and he drew a deep breath to answer the call.

Jack interposed quickly. "Stop! The natives will be down on us soon enough without that. Off with you, old fellow, and fetch our party back. I'll wait here."

Already Don was racing down the side passage. Presently Jack heard him utter a cautious "hullo." A short silence followed; then the echoes told him that the fugitives were hastily retracing their steps. At the same moment a confused uproar burst on his ears from the direction of the chamber in his rear. The pursuing mob had turned the angle of the passage; were actually in sight. The chain attached to Jack's leg clanked impatiently. He fairly danced with excitement. That ill-advised move on the part of the blacks had almost proved fatal to their sole chance of escape.

But not quite; for now Don and the blacks came up, Jack joined them, and, with the oncoming thunder of many feet loud in their ears, away they sped, running as they alone can run who know that death is at their heels.

Two circumstances favoured them so long as the race was confined to the cramped limits of the corridors: the smallness of their own number, and the multitude of their pursuers. Where four could run with ease, forty wasted their breath in fighting each other for running room.

"We must put the pit between us and these howling demons while they're tumbling over each other in the passage here," cried Don.

It was their only hope. Racing on by Jack's side, close on the heels of the blacks, he rapidly explained to his chum—who knew nothing of the pit, having been brought into the rock by a more circuitous route—the nature of the contemplated manœuvre; and gave Spottie and Puggles their instructions how to act, backed up by a wholesome threat of summary abandonment to the enemy should they shirk when it came to the crucial point, the plank. The blacks were to cross first, Jack next; while he, Don, would cover their retreat as best he could. To this arrangement Jack could raise no demur. He was too seriously handicapped by the chain.

A final spurt, and they cleared the tunnel and reached the pit. The plank lay where they had left it. Across it ran their only road to safety. At a significant signal from Don Spottie led off, and, when he had reached the further side in safety, Puggles followed in his tracks. Don's threat, coupled with the ominous uproar belched forth by the mouth of the tunnel, eclipsed all fear of the crocodiles.

"Now, Jack," cried Don, ere the plank had ceased to vibrate under Puggles's tread, "after you."

Jack crossed, and Don was in the act of stepping on the unstable bridge, when the foremost of the native gang burst from the gallery. One swift backward glance—a glance that showed him how alarmingly narrow was the margin between escape and capture — and with outstretched arms he balanced himself on the handbreadth of plank—it was scarcely more—and began the perilous passage. Swift as was this backward glance, it sufficed to show him, too, that the leader of the pursuit was none other than the escaped lascar; and ere he had traversed half the plank's length, he felt it yield and rebound beneath the quick tread of the fellow's feet. At the same instant Jack raised a warning shout.

There are moments when the strongest nerve quails, the steadiest head swings a little off its balance, the surest foot slips. Such a moment did this prove for Don. The disconcerting vibration of the plank, the knowledge that the lascar was at his very back, Jack's sudden shout—these for an instant conspired against and overcame his natural cool-headedness. He made a hurried step or two, staggered, and, his foot catching in the rope where it encircled the plank a short distance from the end, he stumbled and fell.

Fell! but in falling dislodged the end of the plank which lay behind him, and on which the lascar stood, from its hold upon the further brink of the pit. The lascar, throwing up his arms with a despairing shriek, plunged headlong into the pool, where he was instantly seized upon by the ravenous crocodiles and torn limb from limb.

And now, if ever, did the "Providence that sits up aloft" watch over Don. Almost miraculously, as it seemed, instead of plunging into the horrible death-trap below, he fell astride the plank, the hither end of which still retained its hold upon the rock at an angle of perhaps sixty-five degrees; and up this steep incline—whither Bosin had already preceded him — with Jack's assistance he managed to scramble. Then they laid hold upon the plank and dragged it from the pit, amid the furious howling of the baffled rabble debouching from the tunnel opposite.

"Safe over, at any rate," panted Don. "But—good heavens! what's become of the lascar?" For, suspended as he had been between life and death, he had neither heard the lascar's shriek nor witnessed the horrible manner in which he had received his quietus at the jaws of the crocodiles.

Jack pointed out a bright crimson blotch on the surface of the pool. "We've seen the last of him, poor devil," said he with a shudder. "Say, did I tell you—no, of course I didn't—that this fellow's not *my* lascar?"

"What, not the lascar who's been hounding us all this time?"

THE CROCODILE PIT.

"The lascar who's been hounding us on the island here—yes; but not the one who tried to brain me on board the cutter and got the knife for his pains. *That* chap kicked the bucket shortly after he got ashore; this fellow's his brother. They're as like as two peas."

Don vented his astonishment in a shrill whistle.

"Then that accounts for it," said he; "for there being no scar on his shoulder, I mean."

"Precisely; and it came jolly near accounting for yours truly as well," said Jack, with a queer little laugh and a significant shrug of the shoulders. "This fellow, you see—the one who was just now eaten by the crocodiles—raised a sort of vendetta against us when his brother died, and of course he wanted to try his hand on me first, since it was I who gave his brother his death-blow. He'd have done it, too, if it hadn't been for old Salambo. But the old man put his foot down—I overheard their talk last night, and that's how I know—and said he wouldn't allow any violence, lucky for me. He was hoping for overtures from you, I suppose. But I say, what's this about the scar? How do *you* know there was none on the fellow's shoulder?"

"How do I know? Why, you see, it was this way. I was swimming the creek yesterday morning—you shall hear how that came about later on, by the way—when the lascar," indicating the crimson blotch on the pool, "tried to throttle me. I had to knock him on the head to quiet him. Then I towed him ashore, and the captain and I——"

"The captain!" cried Jack with a start. "By Jove, we've left him behind!"

The wild hurry-scurry and excitement of the last half-hour had afforded Don scant opportunity for speaking of the captain's sad end—had, indeed, driven all thought of the old sailor from his mind, as it also had from Jack's. Now that the captain was mentioned, however, Jack, naturally enough, jumped to the conclusion that he had formed one of the rescue party, and had been overlooked in their recent precipitate flight. The time was now come when he must be undeceived; but when Don attempted to disclose the sad truth emotion choked his utterance, and he could not. But Jack, gazing into his convulsed face, instinctively read there what his lips refused to utter.

"When did it happen?" he asked in a hushed, awed whisper. "And how?"

Controlling his voice with an effort, "Only last night," faltered Don; "the lascar did it."

Jack turned away and buried his face in his hands.

"He was strangled," Don presently resumed, "strangled with that cord you see tied to the rope there. Afterwards, when the lascar gave me the slip, as he did in the night, he took the cord with him; but Bosin somehow recovered it and fetched it back. I little guessed how it would serve the lascar out when I used it to bridge the pit!"

"Retribution!" cried Jack, flinging his hands impulsively away from his face. "He's rightly served, the villain. Only "—regretfully—" I wish it had been me instead of the cord, that's all. But it's done, anyhow, so let's get out of this."

And it was time; for during this conversation the natives had not been idle. At this very moment, indeed, a number of them rushed shouting from the tunnel, bearing other planks with which to bridge the chasm. Don and his chum did not wait to see this done. Without further loss of time they set out for the creek, in which direction the blacks had already preceded them.

Hardly had they entered the tunnel, however, when they encountered the blacks, running back full pelt; and before Don could inquire the cause of their precipitate return, a shout, reverberating up the vaulted corridor from the semi-darkness ahead, made inquiry unnecessary. While he and Jack had dallied in fancied security, the natives, skirting the pit by another route, had cut off their retreat.

And, as if to increase the consternation caused by this discovery, at the same instant a chorus of yells in their rear announced that the party in pursuit had succeeded in bridging the pit anew.

CHAPTER XIX.

ONE-TO-TWENTY GIVES TWENTY-TO-ONE THE WORST OF IT.

"HEMMED in!" cried Don, as the desperate character of the situation flashed upon him. "Shall we try to cut our way through the gang ahead, or fall back on the pit?"

"Back!" was Jack's prompt rejoinder. "Once prevent the niggers in our rear from crossing the pit, and we're all right. We'll have more fighting room there, anyhow."

Back they ran, hustling the blacks before them. At the pit matters were even worse than they had feared. Half-a-dozen planks already spanned the chasm, each of them black with natives, who jostled each other in their eagerness to cross, supremely indifferent to the reptilian horrors that awaited them should they lose their balance.

"Hurrah!" shouted Jack, pouncing upon the

bobbing end of the nearest plank. "Tumble 'em in! To the crocodiles with the beggars!"

Though the occupants of the plank could understand not a syllable of Jack's speech, they readily understood his intention; and crowding back upon each other with warning cries, by their combined weight they hastened the very catastrophe they desired to avert. The plank bent like a bow, snapped in twain, and launched its shrieking burden into the abyss. In their frantic efforts to escape, a number of the doomed wretches clutched at a second plank that happened to lie within reach. Already heavily overloaded, this also gave way, and added its quota to the horrible commotion of the pool. Two planks were thus accounted for.

Meanwhile Don and the blacks had not been slow to second Jack's efforts. By their united strength a third plank was dislodged, and they were in the act of attacking the fourth when their energies were diverted into another channel.

For at this juncture the detachment of natives who had cut off the retreat to the creek suddenly appeared upon the scene. The remaining planks, too, now began to pour the enemy upon the hither side of the pit in steady streams.

P 2

The rocky shelf that here flanked the chasm had, perhaps, a width of three yards, and that portion of it to the left of the creek-tunnel's mouth, where the unmolested planks lay, was speedily packed with natives, armed with formidable pikes and knives, who bore down upon the little group with furious outcries and all the weight of superior numbers. Jack was the first to perceive the danger.

"To the right! It's all up with us if we're surrounded."

Suiting the action to the words, he darted to the right, closely followed by Don and the blacks. Here they stationed themselves side by side, the timid blacks in the rear, and prepared to meet their assailants.

"Couldn't be better!" was Jack's cheerful comment, as he took a hasty survey of their surroundings. "Wall on our right; pit on left; enemy in front; and elbow-room behind. Say, we'll buckle to with the muskets first, and reserve the cutlasses till it comes to close quarters. Look out; they're coming!"

On came the howling, disorderly mob, maddened by the terrible fate of their comrades, and thirsting for vengeance.

"Ready!"

Together the muskets rose to the level.

"Don't fire too high. Now, let 'em have it hot!"

The walls of the narrow enclosure rocked with the thunderous report. The mob quailed, fell back; they had no stomach for cold lead.

"That's all right," said Jack coolly as they rapidly reloaded; "but I wish we had breech-loaders! A ball, quick!"

The human wave in front, silent except for a sullen murmur that only waited for the rush to be renewed ere it swelled into fury, was again raising its ugly, threatening crest.

"I doubt if we check it this time," said Don, watching it with anxious eyes; "they've seen us reload, and know where they have the advantage. Better get your cutlass——"

"Ready!" cried his companion.

The wave broke. A hoarse roar, a tumultuous rush such as it seemed no human power could withstand, and it was upon them. Again the walls leapt to the thunder of the muskets; again the serried ranks quailed. But before the smoke had left the muzzles of the muskets, the wave swept on again with redoubled fury, poured itself upon and around the brave lads, swept them off their feet. For a moment it seemed as if the death-balance must kick the beam.

But the "final tussle" was not to be just yet. Spottie and Puggles, terrified into momentary daring by the imminence of their own danger, now threw themselves into the fray with an energy which, if it did little execution, at least served to divert many a blow from their masters. No mean help that—to take the blows meant for another.

Nor were the masters themselves slow to recognise and profit by this fact. Right and left they slashed, dealing terrific swinging blows when they could get them in, lunging desperately at the sinewy, half-naked forms about them when they could not, until British pluck and British muscle told, as they ever must in a righteous struggle for life and liberty, and One-to-twenty found itself clear of the *mêlée*, with a ghastly ridge of wounded at its feet, and fighting room behind.

Well they had it! For the space of one deep breath the disconcerted rabble suspended hostilities, as if unable to believe that Twenty-to-one had got the worst of it. Then their ranks closed up into a solid mass of dusky, perspiring, blood-stained forms, and the onslaught was renewed — not hurriedly now, but with a watchful determination, a guarded fierceness, that forced One-to-twenty back foot by foot until but little room was left for fighting, and none, in sooth, for quarter when it should come, as soon it must, to the sheer wall and the bitter end.

Once more the blacks had slunk to the rear—had, in fact, already reached the wall, where, since they could get no farther, they cowered in miserable anticipation of speedy death. The "final tussle" was not far off now. Don and Jack had barely room to swing their cutlasses in. So much of the rocky ledge as might be measured by a single backward stride—only that separated them from the wall and the last scene of all. Inch by inch, their teeth hard set, their breath coming and going in quick, laboured gasps, they contested this narrow selvage of life. So the balance hung, when there came a second momentary lull in the deadly game of give and take. The dusky foe could now afford to breathe, being confident of the issue.

Keeping a wary eye upon their movements, Don seized his chum by the hand. "I never thought it would come to—to this, old fellow," he said huskily; "God knows I didn't!"

Jack swallowed hard several times before he

could trust himself to reply. "No more did I. But we're not going to funk now, old fellow; and —and I'm glad it's to be together, anyhow!"

One mute, agonised look into each other's eyes; one last pressure of the hand, and again, shoulder to shoulder, they faced the foe and the inevitable end.

At this instant, when it seemed that not a ghost of a chance remained, there arose on their immediate right a shrill chattering sound—a sound that, somehow, had in it a ring of joyousness so strangely out of keeping with the situation that Don turned with a start and a sudden thrill of hope towards the quarter whence it came. As he did so, his eyes fell upon Bosin, forgotten in the heat of the fray, and now perched—good God! upon what?

Don clutched his companion's arm and pointed with unsteady finger.

"Look!"

CHAPTER XX.

THE LAST STRAW.

A GLANCE—more he did not dare bestow whilst confronted by that treacherous throng—showed Jack what he and Don had hitherto entirely failed (and no wonder!) to observe. In the extreme corner of the ledge on which they stood, a deep, narrow gash divided the towering side wall, and up this, clear to the summit of the rock, there ran a flight of steps. On these Bosin had perched himself. At their foot crouched the blacks, blind to everything except their own danger.

"Wake those niggers up, and start them on ahead up the steps!" said Jack quickly. "Look sharp! they're going to rush us again."

Falling on Spottie and Puggles, by dint of vigorous cuffing and shoving Don succeeded in getting them on the stairs. Rapidly as this was done, it produced an instantaneous effect upon the native rabble. They too had overlooked the existence of the stairway until Don's action recalled it to mind. A moment later the opening was besieged by a clamouring, infuriated throng.

"Up with you, old fellow!" cried Jack, turning on the natives with drawn cutlass after he had ascended some half-dozen steps, and thus covering his friend's retreat. "You had your innings at the pit; now it's my turn."

Stationed on the steps as he was, Jack would have possessed no mean advantage over the natives but for one circumstance. The chain attached to his leg dangled down the steps, and the natives, discovering this, promptly seized it. In a twinkling Jack was dragged back into the midst of the furious rabble.

Don was half-way up the steps when the uproar caused by this mishap reached his ears. He turned just in time to see his companion disappear.

Down the steps he bounded, clearing half-a-dozen at a leap, until barely that number lay between him and the bottom, where, owing to Jack's desperate resistance, the natives had their hands too full to notice his approach. Gauging the distance with his eye, he took a flying leap from this height into the very midst of them, scattering them in all directions. As he intended, he overleapt his friend, who now quickly regained his feet. Before the natives had time to recover from the shock of Don's precipitate arrival in their midst, he and Jack were well up the steps again. One or two of the gang made as if to follow them, but turned tail when menaced with the cutlasses.

"Nick and go that time!" cried Don, as he gained the top and threw himself exhausted upon the rock. "Just for a minute I thought it was all U.P."

"Me too," said Jack, with more gravity than grammar; "and, between ourselves, the sensation wasn't half pleasant, either. But, I say, are you hurt?"

"No; nothing worse than a scratch or two. And you?"

"Oh, I'm all right. Though it's little short of a miracle that we weren't spitted on those beastly pikes. Say, do you think they'll try to rush us here?"

"Hardly, after the lesson we've taught them; unless, indeed, there is a wider approach to the summit here than those steps. We ought to look about us at once so as to make sure."

"Right you are," assented Jack. "Let's load the muskets and leave the niggers in charge here while we take our bearin's like, as the captain used to say, poor old chap!"

But when it came to charging the muskets— old-fashioned muzzle loaders, it will be remembered—they made an unpleasant discovery. Don had lost his powder-flask in the fight.

To make matters worse, Spottie, when called upon to produce his, confessed that he had left it on board the cutter in the hurry of the start. Only Pug's flask remained; but this, unfortunately, was nearly empty. There was barely enough powder left for three charges.

This was but one of a series of disconcerting revelations which quickly followed the loading of the muskets.

In the first place, the most careful search failed to disclose any other means of egress from the Rock. In all the length and breadth of its summit they could find no opening except the one by which they had ascended, while on every hand its sides fell away in declivities so steep and smooth that not even Bosin could have found a foothold upon them—or in perpendicular precipices that made the head swim as one looked down from their dizzy height upon the town, or sands, or jungle, far below.

With the bright sky above, and the free air of heaven all around them, they were as effectually hemmed in as when that bristling array of pikes forced them back to the blank wall. The jaws of the trap were a little wider; the effects of its deadly grip a little delayed—that was all.

To add to the horrors of their position, absolute starvation stared them in the face in the event of a prolonged siege. Since early morning they had eaten nothing, and the day was now far advanced; they had brought no food with them, and none was procurable here. A small temple crowned the Rock; but when they penetrated it in the hope of finding fruit or other edible offerings, its dust-laden shrine spoke only too plainly of long disuse. Even the thin clusters of dates upon the few palms that eked out a stunted existence in a shallow depression of the Rock were acrid, shrivelled, and wholly unfit for food. The pit, it is true, contained water; but this, even had it been drinkable, lay hopelessly beyond their reach.

"No powder, no grub, no drink; it's a pretty

pickle to be in, anyhow," said Jack, ruefully summing up these calamitous discoveries as they rejoined the blacks at the head of the stairs. "And, by Jove!" pointing down the steps, "they've gone and doubled the guard."

"The water's the worst," he presently resumed, scanning the arid expanse of rock thirstily. "We could hold out for days, if we only had a supply of that. As it is, I don't dare think what this place will be like under a midday sun—ugh!"

"All the more reason we should leave it, then," said Don.

"How?"

Don was silent. The question did not seem to admit of an answer.

"Now, see here, old fellow," said Jack; "I admit, of course, that U.P. is written large all over the face of things just now; but at the same time it strikes me there's more than one way of getting off our white elephant's back."

"There's only the tunnel to the creek," said Don, "and that's not going to help us much while it's chock-full of natives, and we have no powder."

"Then why not go over the cliff?" demanded Jack.

This daring and seemingly absurd proposal Don greeted with a stare of utter incredulity. " That would be facing death with a vengeance," was his far from encouraging comment. " How high do you estimate the cliff to be, anyway ? "

" A couple of hundred feet or so."

Don laughed. " You may as well say thousands, so far as our chances of reaching the base in safety are concerned. The thing's a sheer impossibility, I tell you; Bosin himself couldn't do it. You're downright mad to think of it, Jack."

" Am I ? I admit the difficulty, but not the impossibility. What Bosin can't do, we can."

" How, I should like to know ? "

" By making a rope. See here, did you notice those palm-trees we passed while making the round of the Rock ? "

"I did; but 'pon my word I don't see what they've got to do with your proposal. Ropes don't grow on palm-trees."

" Oh, but they do, though. Do you mean to say that you never saw the natives make a rope out of the branches of a palm ? "

" Of course I have. And what's more, I know how it's done. But say," his tone suddenly changing to one of anxiety, "suppose the palm-leaves don't give us enough material?"

"I'm not sure they will," said Jack doubtfully, "unless we spin it out pretty fine; and that, of course, increases the danger of breakage. Well, if we run short, we can make shift with the blacks' clothes and turbans. But it's going to take a jolly long time to make—though we ought to finish it easily by to-morrow night. Then, ho for the cliff! And now, old fellow, just lie down, will you, and take a snooze: you're completely done up. When the moon rises I'll call you, and we'll have a whack at the trees, while Pug and Spottie do sentry-go."

The blacks, poor fellows, were already sound asleep, with Bosin snuggled up between them; and Don was not long in following them into that realm of dreams, where waking cares, if they intrude at all, more often than not lie low and shadowy on the horizon. So Jack was left alone in the darkness and solitude of the Rock.

Kicking off his shoes, and tucking the end of the chain beneath his belt to secure perfect noiselessness of movement, he shouldered a musket, and fell to pacing back and forth past the black orifice that marked the point where the stairway cleft the rocky floor. Monotonous work it was, and weird. The steely glint of the stars, the mournful sobbing of the surf upon the sands, sent an involuntary shiver through his frame. He crept softly to the extreme brink of the chasm and peered into its depths. Below all was pitchy blackness; he could distinguish nothing, save, far down, at an infinite depth as it seemed, the faint, fantastic reflection of a star on the surface of the pool. Occasionally a sound of lazy splashing floated up to where he stood, and he thought with creeping flesh of the horrible, ghoulish surfeit the crocodiles had had that day.

To and fro beneath the steely stars—tramp, tramp, tramp, to the solemn dirge of the sea. Would the laggard moon never rise and put an end to his weird vigil?

Hark! what was that? He paused and listened with suspended breath, his back towards the dim outline of the stairway; listened, but heard only the moaning of the surf and the regular, sonorous breathing of his sleeping companions.

"One of those gorged crocodile beasts got a nightmare," he muttered, with a smile at the comic aspect of his own fancy. "Ha," catching sight of a faint, silvery glow in the east, "there's the moon at last. Time to call our fellows; I've had enough of this death's watch, anyhow."

While uttering these words he made a step forward with the intention of calling Don and the blacks, when something whizzed swiftly through the air, he felt a sharp twinge, an intense burning sensation in his left arm, a deathly faintness stealing over him, and realised that he was wounded—wounded by a dexterously-thrown knife, which, had it not been for that timely forward stride, must have buried itself deep in his back. Luckily, in spite of the pain and giddiness, he retained his presence of mind. Quick as a flash he wheeled, brought the hammer of the musket to full cock, and the musket itself to his shoulder. Above the yawning staircase the outline of a human figure showed indistinctly.

"One for you," muttered Jack, and fired.

The figure threw up its arms and fell backwards.

The report of the musket brought Don to his feet. "What's the row?" he asked, running to his companion's side in alarm.

The appearance of other figures in lieu of the first supplied a more pertinent answer to this question than Jack could have given. He snatched up one of the remaining muskets, Jack possessing himself of the other. By this time Spottie and Puggles were also up, but, like the dutiful servants they were, they kept well in the rear of their masters.

The enemy were now literally swarming up the steps and sides of the stairway.

Jack gave the word—" Blaze away ! " and a double report went hurtling wildly out over the sea.

Clubbing their muskets, they then fell upon and began clubbing the escaladers with an energy that speedily choked the contracted avenue of approach to the summit of the Rock with a heaving, scrambling, trampling mass of natives, whose desperate struggles to regain their lost foothold upon the steps only served to facilitate their descent to the bottom. In five minutes' time the repulse was complete ; the foe retreated into the dark security of the chasm, leaving some six or eight of their number lying upon the scene of the affray. Jack threw aside his musket and sprang down the steps to where they lay.

" What are you after now ? " cried Don, leaping down after him.

" Cloths," was Jack's laconic rejoinder, as he

unceremoniously began to divest the natives of the long strips of country cotton that encircled their waists. "We want these for our rope."

On hearing this Don also set to work, and in a short time they had secured some half-dozen cloths, together with an equal number of turbans, which lay scattered all up and down the steps like enormous mushrooms. With this booty they returned in triumph to the summit of the rock.

"They'll average twelve feet at least," said Jack, eyeing the tumbled heap critically. "Let's see—twelve twelves make a hundred and forty-four; and by tearing them in two down the middle we'll get double length. Total, two hundred and eighty-eight feet. Hurrah, we've got our rope!"

"And a far safer one," observed Don, "than if we had patched it up out of those palm-leaves. Well, it's an ill wind that——"

He got no further, for Jack suddenly dropped at his feet as though he had been shot. He had fainted from loss of blood, as Don, to his horror, quickly discovered. As a matter of fact, the knife that had penetrated Jack's arm was still in the wound, and its projecting hilt was the first intimation Don received of his chum's hairbreadth escape. By the time he had removed the knife, ripped open the coat-sleeve, and bandaged the wound with a fragment torn from one of the cloths, Jack opened his eyes.

"Why didn't you tell me about this?" exclaimed Don reproachfully. "How did it happen?"

"How? Oh, one of those treacherous niggers shot his knife at me—the old trick," said Jack, scrambling to his feet and shaking himself with nonchalant air. "I'd have told you, only I forgot it in the scuffle. Nothing but a scratch, anyway; I'm all right."

Don's look was rather dubious, for, in spite of his companion's assumption of *sang-froid*, he could not but foresee the possible effect of a badly-wounded arm upon their proposed descent of the cliff.

The moon was now well above the horizon; so, setting the blacks to watch the stairs, they went to work on the rope at once—an easy task compared to what it must have been had they attempted to utilise the tough, fibrous palm-branches, as at first proposed.

"You haven't told me yet," Jack presently observed, pausing in his task of knotting together the long strips of cloth as Don tore them off ready to his hand; "you haven't told me how you came to lay the lascar by the heels—in the creek, I think you said? Let's have the story now, old fellow."

"Oh, there's a whole cable's-length of events leading up to that," said Don. "I'd better begin at the beginning — with your disappearance, I mean."

So there, beneath the stars, while the rope which was to ensure escape from the Rock grew under their busy fingers, he recounted link by link the chain of events which the days and nights of Jack's absence had forged.

Far into the night did the story spin itself out, for Jack had many questions to ask, many comments to make; until at last it came to that terrible moment when Don had sought to rouse the captain, and found him to be sleeping the sleep that knows no waking. His voice grew choked and husky then; Jack bent low over his work, and tears glistened in the ghostly moonlight.

"And in his jacket pocket I found this," concluded Don, producing the well-thumbed Prayer Book. "On the fly-leaf — no, you can't make it out now, the light is so faint — but on the fly-leaf the dear old chap had written that whatever happened, he was to be buried at sea. So this morning, just before daybreak, we put off in the cutter, and gave him what he wished for—a seaman's burial."

Jack knew the whole sad story now, and for a time they fell into one of those silences which, somehow, are apt to follow the mention of the dead who have endeared themselves to us in life —silences eloquent, in their very stillness, of regret and grief.

"There, it's done," said Jack at last, as he tied and tested the final knot. "And now, hurrah for the cliff!"

Don had begun to coil the rope, when he suddenly paused in his task and exclaimed:

"Say, how are we going *to fasten the end?*"

"Fasten the end? Why, to——" Jack came to an abrupt stop, adding blankly after a moment: "Blest if I know what we *can* fasten it to!"

"Nor I," Don acknowledged, as much taken aback as his companion by the appalling nature of this discovery. "There are the palms, of course, and the temple; but they're too far from the cliff to be of any use. The rope will hardly reach as it is, I'm afraid."

"Oh, there must be some way of securing it," replied Jack incredulously. "Surely there's a crack or something we can wedge one of the cutlasses into. Let's look, anyhow!"

Look they did, but not with the result Jack had so confidently anticipated. From side to side, from end to end of the Rock, they searched and searched again, even going down on their hands and knees that they might perchance feel what had escaped the eye. But without avail. So far as the moonlight enabled them to discern —and it made the place nearly as light as day— neither crack nor projection marred the smooth surface of the stone. They gave it up at length, utterly disheartened. Even Jack felt this to be the last straw, and abandoned himself to despair.

"It's a bad job altogether," was the despondent comment with which he threw himself down beside the apparently useless coil of rope. "God help us, we haven't a ghost of a chance left!"

"Oh, things aren't quite so bad as that!"

replied his companion, with an assumption of hopefulness he was far from feeling. "Who can say what may turn up? The darkest hour is just before the dawn, you know."

"But," said Jack, "suppose there isn't any dawn, what then?"

CHAPTER XXI.

RIVALS FOR THE HONOURS OF DEATH.

A NIGHT of dread foreboding, of weary watching for the day that seemed as if it would never come. With what tantalising slowness did the snail-like stars crawl across the black vault of the heavens! And when day came, what then?

Hunger and thirst, danger and despair, and the certainty of death! But no need to await the dawn for these; already they were here. Comfortable bed-fellows, truly, and for a bed the bare, unyielding rock.

Jack lay with his head pillowed upon the coil of rope. Not that he found it a comfortable resting-place. The knowledge of what the rope could *not* do for them made it a pillow of thorns. He could not rest. The last thread of hope had broken, plunging him into the abyss of despair. Besides, his arm had become extremely painful within the last hour; he was restless, feverish. Fever goads the brain. Jack's brain was just then busier, perhaps, than it had ever been before. He felt none of the sharp gnawings of hunger, none of the insatiable cravings of thirst, though, as a matter of fact, these were even then conspiring with his wound to fever his blood and keep him awake, and make him think, think, think with never an instant's pause. When thought is goaded like this, it speedily verges on delirium.

To give way to despondency was not at all like Jack; and as he tossed from side to side and thought upon the "whine" (that was what he called it, in his own mind) in which he had indulged a little while ago when the utter desperateness of the situation first burst upon him—when he thought of this, he felt heartily ashamed of himself. He was a coward, a rank, out-and-out coward. He hated himself for his faint-hearted, babyish lack of spirit. But he would redeem his reputation yet. He would show them—meaning Don and the blacks—that he was no coward, anyhow!

The blacks, as they crossed and recrossed each other on their noiseless beat, thought little and said less. They were desperately hungry, and hunger is the one fellow-feeling that does not make us wondrous kind. Every now and then they tightened their waist-cloths a little, but beyond this gave no outward sign or token of what they thought or felt.

So the night wore on, and still Jack thought in restless silence. There was a deeper flush on his cheek, but it was no longer the flush of shame. The fever in his blood, the delirium in his brain, were rising. So was his resolution. He flung himself about restlessly, muttering. He would show them he was no coward, anyhow!

So the night wore on, until by-and-by, as Don turned for the hundredth time upon his uneasy couch—for he, too, was unable to rest—his hand came into accidental contact with that of his chum. He started; Jack's hand was fiery hot.

Roused by his companion's touch and movement, Jack sat bolt upright, and gazed about him in an excited, feverish fashion, muttering incoherently. His breath came and went in short, hurried catches, and in his eyes shone an unnatural wildness that struck terror to Don's heart. Knowing nothing of his chum's resolve, he thought him simply delirious.

"Lie down," he said soothingly, placing his

hand on Jack's shoulder, and attempting, with gentle force, to push him back into his former recumbent position.

Jack flung the hand aside petulantly. Whatever of delirium there might be in his eyes and manner, his words, though spoken rapidly and with excitement, were rational enough.

"Look here, old fellow," he cried, "it's all my fault, your being here in this fix; and I'm bound to do my level best to get you safe out of it, especially after the way I funked a while back. No, don't cut in and try to stop me—I know what I'm saying right enough, though I expect I do look a bit wild and that. Now, my arm here—I ain't said much about it—'tain't like me to whine, anyhow—at least not often—but all the same, my arm's getting jolly bad. Knotting the rope and that, you see, has made it a bit worse, and—well, the fact is, old fellow, I don't believe I could go down that rope to save my neck, even supposing it to be fastened, you understand."

"I feared as much," said Don gravely.

"Yes? Well, that's just how it stands," Jack went rapidly on. "'Tisn't that I'm afraid, you understand—there's no cliff hereabouts that would make me funk—it's simply that my arm's out of gear and won't work. Not even if the rope were fastened, you see, which it isn't. And that's what I'm coming at, old fellow. Look here, I'll tell you what we *can* do. Spottie and Pug can lower you away—over the cliff, you know—and then, when Pug and I have sent Spottie after you, I'll manage somehow to pay out the line while Pug follows. He's the lightest weight of the lot, anyhow."

"All very well," demurred Don, who thought he saw a fatal objection to Jack's plan, "but how will you get down yourself?"

"Oh, my getting down isn't in the bill at all," said Jack; "I mean to stay right here."

This announcement fairly took Don's breath away. He had supposed all along that Jack was holding the pith of his proposal in reserve; but never once had he so much as dreamed of such a climax as this.

"What! stop here?" he gasped. "You don't know what you're saying—it's certain death."

"Hope I ain't such a duffer as not to know that," said Jack brusquely. "All the same, I mean to stay."

"Don't say that, Jack."

"Why not? Better one than four."

"Then I'll stop with you," said Don, with dogged determination. "The blacks may have my chance and welcome. Nothing on earth will induce me to go."

His chum was silent for a long time after that —so long, indeed, that Don thought the matter settled for good and all. But in this he was mistaken.

"Say, old fellow," said Jack at last, "tell you what I'll do; I'll toss you as to which of us is to go. What do you say?"

"No, no," cried Don.

"But why not? Where's the use of being such a softie over the matter? There are no end of reasons why I should stay, I tell you. For one thing, I've got no mother to consider."

"That's true enough," assented Don, gulping as he thought of his own mother.

"And no sisters or brothers."

"Don't," said Don huskily; "you forget me, Jack."

"No, I don't," protested Jack; "you are more to me than any brother could ever be, old man; but that's only an additional reason why I should see you safe out of this mess. Then there's another thing; you know how good the guv has always been to me—sent me to school, and treated me just as if I was his own son, you know."

"Yes?" said Don.

"Well, I've always felt that if ever I got the chance I should like to repay his kindness, don't you know; and now that the chance has come I don't mean to let it slip. Say, will you toss?"

Don wavered. It seemed terribly hard that they should all have to die like so many rats in a trap. Besides, once he and the blacks were off the Rock, they could fall back on the cutter, renew their stock of ammunition, and——

"I'll toss you on one condition," he said suddenly.

"What condition's that?"

"Why, this. That after the die is cast we take no further steps until daylight, so as to make quite sure there's no way of securing the rope to the rock. Are you agreed?"

For reply Jack held out his hand, and thus the compact was sealed. Then Don drew a rupee from his pocket and passed it to his companion.

"Tails, you go," said Jack, and tossed.

A flash of silver in the moonlight, a mocking jingle, and the coin lay still. Eagerly the rivals for the honours of death bent over it.

"Tails!"

"I knew it!" said Jack quietly; "and what's more, I'm jolly glad it isn't heads."

His chum turned quickly away and bowed his head upon his knees, while a sound suspiciously like a stifled sob broke the stillness of the night. Jack crept close up to him and slipped an arm about his neck. So, for a long time, they sat in silence.

CHAPTER XXII.

A REPORT FROM THE SEA.

JACK was the first to break the silence that followed the spinning of the fateful coin. He rose, stretched himself, and, pointing to a ruddy glow that had begun to light up the eastern horizon, exclaimed in a voice of undisguised relief:

"Daybreak at last!"

"I only wish it would never come," his companion rejoined gloomily, turning his gaze upon the unwelcome light—of which, however, he had caught scarce a glimpse ere he sprang to his feet in sudden excitement.

"That's no daybreak, Jack! It's more like the reflection of a fire."

"I believe you're right," assented Jack. "It certainly *is* a fire; but where can it be, that we see only the reflection? Behind Haunted Pagoda Hill?"

"No; this side of the hill, I should say."

"Then it must be somewhere in the creek."

At mention of the creek Don started violently, a suspicion of the truth flashing upon him. He began to sniff the air. An odour of smoke floated to them on the fresh morning breeze, faint but pungent. Jack, catching a whiff of it, fell to sniffing too.

"Well, what do you make of it?" Don inquired anxiously.

"Tar!" replied Jack, without hesitation.

"I thought so," said Don, with a queer catch in his voice. "Jack, it's the cutter!"

With this he set off at a run towards that part of the Rock which overlooked the creek. Advancing as far as the rapidly-increasing slope of the declivity made it prudent to venture, he came to a stand. The glow of the fire was now brighter, though its source still remained hidden from view; but by edging his way well to the right, he at length succeeded in reaching a point whence the ruddy light that had excited his fears could be seen as a leaping, swaying column of smoke and flame, terminating, far down amid the darkness of the creek, in a single point of lurid red.

"Just as I feared!" he cried, as Jack rejoined.

him. "The niggers have set fire to the *Jolly Tar*. I was afraid the rascals had smelt her out when I met the lascar in the creek the other morning. The old boat's done for, anyhow; so let me off my promise, Jack."

"What for? I can't see that the burning of the cutter has anything to do with it. There are plenty of native boats to get away in."

"Oh, it isn't the getting away! You don't suppose I'd go off and leave you in the lurch, I hope? It's the powder that troubles me. There wasn't much on board the cutter, it's true; just about enough to fight my way back here with— as I meant to do, please God, had this not happened. I planned the whole thing out while we sat mooning yonder, you see. But now!" and at thought of how this hope—the secret of his acquiescence in the outcome of that fatal toss—had vanished into thin air before his very eyes, Don's lips trembled and his voice choked.

"Never mind, old chap!" said Jack, deeply touched by this new proof of his friend's generosity; "I'll take the will for the deed. But, I say—you pledged me your word, you know; and at daybreak, if no way of anchoring the rope shows up, I shall expect you to go over the cliff like a man. We shan't have long to wait now. Look!"

He pointed to a deep roseate hue which tinged the sky just above the ocean rim. And even as they stood watching it, the light came leaping up from the sea, and outshone the stars, and set the whole east aglow. A flush of dawn, and it was day.

"Now," said Jack, tightening his belt, "let's make the round of the Rock again. If there's a shadow of a flaw anywhere we're bound to find it in this light."

"Heaven grant we may!" ejaculated Don, as they began the search.

The cliff forming the Elephant's left side was out of it altogether. The native town lay directly at its base, rendering escape in that direction impracticable. So, too, with that part of the Rock abutting on the creek; its formation was such that no human being, rope or no rope, could have made his way down its face. There remained only the Elephant's right flank — overlooking the jungly back of the island—and the loftier head parts facing the western sea. To these, then, the search was necessarily confined.

Again and yet again did they pace the dizzy

heights, scanning every inch of the rocky surface for that crack or projection upon the existence of which Jack's life was staked. But, as before, the search ended in failure and despair. There was absolutely nothing—neither crevice, nor jutting point, nor friendly block of stone—in which, or to which, the rope's end could be made fast : nothing but Jack's body !

To secure the rope to the palms or the masonry of the temple was an utter impossibility. It was too short by half.

As a last hope Don approached the chasm in which lay the pool. But the hope was short-lived. The native guard had been trebled overnight. Hope—so far, at least, as Jack's life was concerned—stood on a par with the powder: not a grain was left.

As a matter of fact, Don had all along indulged a secret conviction that "something would turn up." Now, when the terrible truth was at last forced upon him in such a manner that he could no longer shut his eyes to it, his distress was pitiable to witness.

He had hazarded his friend's life on the toss of a coin—and lost ! And now he must go over the cliff—over the cliff to safety and life—over the cliff by means of a rope, at the death-end of which stood his dearest friend. Given his choice, he would have taken that friend's place—oh, how gladly! But go he must, for his honour was pledged, and the time was come!

Ay, the time was come—the supreme moment of Jack's heroic resolve. And Jack was glad of it, ready for it. The fever in his blood had abated, leaving him cool, collected, and more firm in his resolve than ever. He had chosen his course and he would stick to it, anyhow!

"Come," he said simply, laying a gentle hand on Don's shoulder, "it is time for us to go."

"For us!" The words, though kindly meant, stabbed Don to the heart.

Kicking the coil of rope before him like a ball, Jack approached the brink of the precipice. The blacks followed. There was little danger of their being missed by the native guard, unless the latter mounted the steps, and this they were not likely to do after the severe lesson they had received in the night. Last of all came Don— slowly, reluctantly. He looked and felt like one going to his execution.

Without a word Jack picked up the loose end of the rope and knotted it securely about his friend's chest, beneath his arms. When he had uncoiled the rope to its full length, he fastened the other end about his own waist. Then he held out his hand.

"Good-bye, old fellow," he said, his voice shaking in spite of himself. "Good-bye, and God bless you! Be sure and cast the rope loose when you reach the ground."

"Oh, Jack, Jack! Must I go — must I?" cried Don desperately, his voice full of agony.

With unfaltering step Jack led him to the extreme brink of the cliff, left him there with his face set towards liberty and life, turned back, and beckoning to the blacks—who had purposely been kept in ignorance of Jack's resolve—prepared to pay out the line.

"Over with you, old fellow! As gently as you can!"

The rope tightened. Wheeling where he stood, Don cast one last imploring look at his friend, who pointed upwards and then motioned him to go. He obeyed.

As the remorseless Rock closed above him, he let himself swing, neither seeing nor caring whither he was being lowered. The abyss below had no terrors for him—he even hoped that the rope

DON GOES DOWN THE CLIFF.

[*Page* 248.

might snap—why should he live since Jack must die? And when at last his feet touched earth, and he had flung the rope from him like a hated thing, he threw himself upon his face at the foot of the insurmountable cliff and burst into a passion of bitter, remorseful tears.

After a time a gentle thud on the back aroused him. He looked up. It was the rope again, but empty! What did it mean? Where was Spottie? Why had he not been sent down? What had happened? A dozen questions such as these flashed through his brain, and with them a sudden wild hope. He started to his feet.

A scrap of paper was secured to the rope by a half-knot. He snatched at it, drawing it to him with something of dread in the movement. It was a leaf from Jack's note-book, scrawled over with writing in Jack's familiar hand. His eyes devoured the words:—

"Good news! A wonderful thing has happened. Was just going to lower Spottie away when the report of a gun came booming up from the sea. The schooner—the governor's schooner —is at anchor off the front of the island! I'd signal her, only I have no powder. I'm all in a daze, anyhow; but you'll know what to do."

An exclamation of intense gratitude to Heaven burst from Don's lips, and crushing the scrap of paper in his hand, he set off at a run along the base of the cliff, in the direction of the Elephant's head.

CHAPTER XXIII.

DON RUNS THE GAUNTLET.

THERE was but one thing to be done: he must gain the schooner with all possible speed, at any risk, and take immediate steps for Jack's rescue.

Instinctively he shaped his course for the Elephant's head. The precipitous cliff was there skirted by a narrow beach. He had seen it gleaming above the surf-line while rounding the island on the morning of their arrival. This beach would afford a short-cut to the front of the island, off which the schooner lay. Once there, he must swim for it. These were his thoughts as he ran.

Tough work it was. True, the jungle did not grow close up to the base of the cliff; but here and there yawning *nullahs*, of considerable depth, and with sides almost as steep as walls, had been cut across his pathway by the rains. At intervals, too, he encountered rugged, irregular heaps of stones, fallen from the cliff above, and studded thick with thorny clumps of prickly-pear.

The cutlass at his side impeded his progress. He threw it away. Then on again.

The sands at last! Close on his right lay the sea, close on his left rose the beetling cliff. There was not much room—just enough to run in. Away before him, like a narrow ribbon of burnished silver, stretched the smooth, hard sands, with never a living thing in sight on all their gleaming reach.

Gradually the cliffs crept behind, and the sea-front opened out before him. And now, of a sudden, he espied a group of natives making for the beach—a company of fishermen, laden with creels, and oars, and nets.

Just ahead, a wedge-shaped gully split the low bank that bordered the beach on the landward side. Above this bank were the fishermen, heading for the gully. They were perhaps fifty yards short of it, while he, on the beach below the bank, was a full hundred. Should they reach it first, he would certainly be intercepted; whereas, could he but pass the point of danger ere the natives gained it, he might succeed in eluding them. They did not see him yet. He darted under the bank, and ran as he had never run in all his life before.

Seventy-five yards, fifty yards, twenty yards—and then the gully. Had the natives reached it? As he raced past he darted a swift sidelong glance at the *nullah*. The fishermen were already half-way down it. They saw him, dropped their fishing implements, and gave chase, yelling like a pack of fiends.

On and on he ran, looking back but once to ascertain what start he had of the dusky gang. Twenty yards at least. They were just emerging from the bottom of the gully.

And now, away to the right, he sighted the schooner, riding at anchor with half a mile of sea between her holding-ground and the shore. He could see her boats swinging at the davits. They had not sighted him, then. He wondered whether Jack could see him from the cliff.

Jack caught sight of Don as he raced past the gully. The fishermen, as it happened, were just then in the gully itself, and consequently invisible. Don's appearance he hailed with a shout.

"Hurrah! he hasn't lost much time, anyhow."

This exclamation brought both Spottie and Puggles to his side in hot haste. The stairs were thus left unguarded—a step the imprudence of which was wholly overlooked in the excitement of the moment.

At sight of his master tearing along the beach below, a grim delight—not unmixed with anxiety—overspread Puggles' black countenance, while a chuckle of intense satisfaction welled up from the red abyss of his fat, shiny throat. Then, like the shadow of an April cloud driven swiftly across a sunlit meadow, a look of blank dismay eclipsed the grin, the chuckle died away in a gasp of alarm, and pointing to the beach with shaking finger, he cried :

"Sar! sar! black warmints done catch um, sar!"

His alarm was well-founded. The fishermen had just tumbled out of the gully, at Don's very heels, as it seemed at this distance.

"They're after him, sure enough," cried Jack. "By Jove, how he runs! Go it, old fellow! you've got the start of them, anyhow."

Away went Don, running like a deer, and after him pelted the fishermen, in a headlong, rough-and-tumble, happy-go-lucky fashion, that, under circumstances less serious, must have provoked the spectators on the Rock to hearty laughter. No laughing matter this, however; for Don's pursuers, having thrown aside their fishing gear, and being moreover fresh in wind and limb, were seen to gain on him at every stride. The race could not prolong itself for many minutes now, and the finish—Jack shuddered as he thought of what that must be.

At this critical juncture, too, matters took an unexpected turn for the worse. A short distance up the beach a second party of natives appeared on the scene. Don ran straight on, apparently not perceiving them. They, on the contrary, saw him, and bore down upon him swiftly. Their cries, doubtless, warned him of his danger, for now he pulled up short, looked ahead, glanced quickly over his shoulder, and then——

With a groan Jack turned away.

A loud outcry from the blacks, however, drew his gaze seawards again, and as he looked his pulses thrilled. Don was making straight for the surf!

As often happens on these coasts when the wind is but a whisper, and the sea glass-like in its placidity, a heavy ground-swell was rolling sullenly in from the outer bay. A stone's throw from the shore this swell was but a sinuous, almost imperceptible, undulation of the glassy surface; but as it swept towards the beach, where the water shoaled rapidly, of a sudden it reared aloft a crest of hissing foam, which curled higher and higher as it came on, until it overtopped the sands at the height of a boat's mast. Then with a mighty roar it broke, hurled itself far up the shelving sands, and retired, seething, to make room for the green battalions pressing shorewards in its wake.

Straight towards this living wall of water Don ran. The two bands of natives, uniting their forces as they swerved aside like bloodhounds in pursuit, were close upon him. Before, above him, curled the mighty wave; and then, to his great horror, Jack saw him stumble and fall.

Lucky fall! Ere the natives could throw themselves upon him, the combing wave broke, passed directly over his prostrate body, swept the niggers off their legs, and hurled them with irresistible force far up the beach.

A moment later the breathless watchers on the cliff saw a black object floating on the surface of the water, yards from shore. It was Don. The under-tow had swept him out to sea, beyond his pursuers' reach.

An expert and powerful swimmer, he lost no time in increasing the distance between himself and the disconcerted native crew, one or two of whom attempted to overtake him, but soon gave it up for a bad job.

Then a boat put off from the schooner, and soon Jack had the satisfaction of seeing his plucky friend hauled in over her side. A quarter of an hour later, when the boat had regained the schooner, the signal gun once more boomed out over the sea, and with feelings of devout thankfulness to Heaven Jack realised that Don was safe on board, and that the term of his own and his companions' imprisonment on the summit of the Rock was bounded by a few brief hours at the most.

Even as he looked, as if by magic the schooner's canvas swelled to the breeze, and he caught the distant song of the lascars as they hove the anchor to the cathead.

Hunger, thirst, his wound, the very enemy at the foot of the rock stairs—all had been forgotten in the breathless interest inspired by Don's race for life; were forgotten still as he and the blacks stood watching the schooner get under weigh.

Till a sharp clank of metal, as of a spear carelessly let fall, recalled their roving thoughts, and brought them swiftly to the right-about, to find the Rock in the immediate vicinity of the pit's mouth literally swarming with armed natives.

CHAPTER XXIV.

IN THE NICK OF TIME.

THE surprise had been cleverly executed. Another moment, and Jack and his black attendants would have been surrounded. As it was, the odds were dead against them.

The unexpected appearance of the schooner had evidently wrought a complete change in the tactics of the enemy. So here they were.

This sleek, corpulent native who led the escaladers was none other than old Salambo! Salambo, the shark-charmer, thief, and director-in-chief of the harassing attacks by which they, the party of adventurers in search of what was indisputably their own, had been baffled at every turn.

By means of the lascar's murderous hand he had clutched at the captain's throat and taken the captain's life. And now that his tool was for ever wrenched from his grasp, he had come in person to add the finishing-stroke to his evil work. Jack's blood boiled as he thought of it. One swift glance around, and his course was taken.

"The temple, Spottie! Point for the temple, Pug!"

The natives, perceiving their intention, swerved aside and attempted to cut them off. But so unexpected was Jack's manœuvre, so prompt the obedience of Spottie and Puggles, that the attempt proved unsuccessful. A wild, breathless dash, and they had turned the corner of the temple—whose door, as usual, faced east — and crossed its threshold.

Old and neglected as the edifice was, stout wooden doors still swung upon the rust-eaten hinges. To slam these to and thrust the bolts home, top and bottom, was the work of but a moment. Bosin darted in as the great doors swung into place, narrowly escaping the amputation of his tail as the penalty of his tardiness. Scarcely had the last bolt been shot when up trooped the enemy, howling like hyenas, and commenced a determined assault upon the doors.

At first they hurled themselves upon the barrier and attempted to force it in by sheer imposition of weight. Thud followed thud in furious succession, while Jack stood by with palpitating heart. His fears as to the stability of the doors, however, were soon set at rest. They creaked, yielded a little, but otherwise stood as firm as the solid masonry in which they were framed. The natives were not slow to discover this, and the ill-advised attempt was soon abandoned. In the brief lull that followed Jack looked about him.

Inside here, beneath the cobwebbed, blackened roof of the outer temple, the light was funereal in its dimness. What little there was crept in through the cracks in the shrunken doors in a reluctant sort of way, as if it found the society of bats and spiders anything but agreeable; except at the further or western end of the temple, where there was a second chamber, smaller and somewhat better lighted than the first. Eight feet or so above the floor a small square window pierced the wall, and directly beneath this stood a sort of stone pediment or shrine, on which squatted a hideously distorted image. This was the temple *swami*, and *swami's* ugly head reached to within a couple of feet of the window.

A second attempt was now made upon the

doors, though not after the haphazard fashion of the first. The cracks in the shrunken woodwork attracting the attention of the natives, they fell to work on the widest of these, and with their spears began chipping away the plank splinter by splinter. But the extreme toughness of the material, seasoned as it was by unnumbered years of exposure to the elements, rendered the task of demolition both difficult and slow.

"Take you a jolly long time to get your ugly head-pieces through that, anyhow!" muttered Jack, as he watched—or rather listened to, for he could see little or nothing of what was going on outside—the fast and furious play of the spears. "And when you do get 'em through, why then——"

To symbolise what would happen then, Jack did what was certainly quite excusable under the circumstances—spat in his palm, and with immense gusto decapitated an imaginary nigger.

Still, given sufficient time for the spears to do their work, it was a foregone conclusion that the doors must fall. Would they hold out till the schooner cast anchor off the creek? He allowed an hour for that—an hour from the time the anchor was weighed. Well, they—he and the two blacks—had been in the temple the best part of an hour already. So that was all right.

But then, the rescue party must make their way up the creek, and from the creek to the summit of the Rock, along that passage by which Don and the blacks had entered on the previous day. This would consume another hour. He made the calculation with the utmost coolness; only, when it was finished, and he asked himself whether the doors would hold out that other hour, the reluctant "No" with which he was compelled to answer the question somehow stuck in his throat and nearly choked him. By way of relief, he slashed the head off another imaginary nigger.

The second hour wore on. The gap in the door grew wider and wider beneath the ceaseless play of the spears, and still the natives showed no signs of desisting or of taking their departure.

Presently a shadow darkened the little window at the rear of the temple. Jack turned on his heel expecting to see a native, but instead saw only Bosin. The monkey had clambered up the image, and so reached the window. The sight of the creature gave Jack a sudden inspiration.

What was to hinder the blacks and himself

from beating a noiseless retreat by way of this same window? The aperture was quite ample in size to admit of their squeezing through it. But — his wounded arm! And could the thing be done without attracting the attention of the gang about the doors?

He climbed up the image and looked out. So far as he could discover the way was clear. Between that end of the temple and the stairs leading to the pit, not a single native was to be seen. True, his view was but limited at the best — the aperture was so narrow, and a straggling blackskin or two might, after all, have their eyes on the window, or, worse still, be guarding the stairs. Probably, though — and this seemed the more likely view — the entire force and attention of the belligerents were concentrated upon the temple doors. He would risk it, anyhow!

Once gain the pit, and they were as good as saved; for by that time the rescue party could not be far off.

A wilder shout from the besiegers recalled his thoughts and eyes to the doors. He scrambled down off the idol's head and ran into the outer chamber.

What was that peculiar crackling sound—this pungent odour with which the air had suddenly grown so heavy? Fire—smoke! They had set fire to the doors!

He ran back into the inner chamber. The blacks were there, cowering in terror against the wall. In a few hurried words he directed them how to proceed. They pulled themselves together and prepared to obey the sahib's directions.

"The window, lads! through the window! Quick now, you lazy beggars!"

Spottie went first—somewhat unwillingly, it must be confessed, which was scarcely to be wondered at, considering that the drop from the window might land him in the arms of the enemy, or on the point of a spear. The smallness of the aperture, its height from the ground, and the necessity for going through it feet foremost, made a triple difficulty, too. But with Jack's assistance this was speedily overcome, and Spottie dropped out of sight. Barring the faint thud of his bare feet on the rock, no sound followed. Thus far, then, the stratagem had escaped detection. Jack began to breathe easier.

After Spottie went Puggles—with even more difficulty, for, as the reader is aware, Puggles was extremely fat ; and again all was still without. Within there was noise enough and to spare. The crackling of the burning doors had grown ominously loud. As Pug's black head disappeared, too, a tremendous shout burst from the rabble gathered about the entrance. Its significance Jack did not stop to inquire. Already he had scaled the image. A wry face or two at the pain of his wounded arm, and a moment later he stood beside the blacks.

The moment of their flight was well chosen. The natives, to a man, were watching the doors with all their eyes.

Bidding the blacks follow close at his heels, he sped across the few yards of rock that separated the temple from the stairs, sprang down the steps, and fell insensible at the feet of his friend, Roydon Leigh.

The rescue party had arrived in the very nick of time.

CHAPTER XXV.

THE SHARK-CHARMER IS CAUGHT IN HIS OWN TRAP.

AFTER all, Jack was but human. His fortitude, strung to a tense pitch by those terrible days and nights of danger, snapped, in presence of actual safety, like an overdrawn bow.

A pitiful spectacle he presented, his clothes torn to ribbons, his hands and face grimy, blood-stained, yet ghastly in their pallor. Don uttered a cry and flung himself on his knees beside his chum. He thought him dead.

"No, not dead, thank God! Only done up. He'll be all right soon," said Captain Leigh, with his hand upon Jack's heart, which still beat, though faintly; and taking out a pocket-flask he poured a few drops of brandy between the drawn, bloodless lips of the unconscious lad.

Under this stimulating treatment Jack soon came round. Needless to dwell on the confusion into which his thoughts were thrown by the sight of the familiar faces bending over him. His bewilderment, however, was but momentary. Memory returned with a rush and spurred him to action and speech. He sat bolt upright.

"Have you got the rascal?" he demanded in eager tones.

"What rascal?" asked Don.

"The shark-charmer, to be sure. Who else should I mean? He's on the Rock, I tell you!"

"Him done stick his leg in trap, sa'b," interpolated Puggles, with appropriate action.

Don started to his feet. Jack followed suit, somewhat unsteadily.

"Is he above there?" cried Captain Leigh.

"Yes, yes!" said Jack eagerly.

"Up with you, boys!" cried the captain to the *peons*.

Don had already acquainted his father with the shark-charmer's part in the tragic events of the past week, and the *peons* had overheard the story. They all knew the shark-charmer, and they followed their leader with enthusiasm. They carried carbines; these glinted in the sunshine, and clanked against the contracted walls of the rock stairway as they jostled each other in the ascent.

A rush of many feet above, and the natives appeared at the stair-head. Only the moment before had they discovered the temple to be deserted, and become alive to the fact that they had lingered too long on the Rock. They were now in hot pursuit of the fugitives. But the sudden apparition of the red-sashed *peons*, the ominous glint and clash of the carbines, promised hotter pursuit than they had bargained for. A wave of consternation swept through their ranks. *Sauve qui peut!* In headlong flight they scattered in all directions.

As before, the shark-charmer had led the gang. He almost ran into the arms of the *peons*.

"Rama! Rama!"

It was the cry of a coward and miscreant who knows that his last hour of freedom, if not of life, has come : the hour of reckoning for his misdeeds.

For as long as it took his half-paralysed tongue to frame the words, the shark-charmer faced his approaching doom. Then he turned and fled like a frightened cur.

The voice of Captain Leigh rang out on the air clear and full as the note of a bugle :

"After him, lads! Never mind the others! Take the fellow alive!"

Up scrambled the *peons* in obedience to the command, deploying to right and left in a long, semicircular line as they debouched upon the Rock.

"Forward!"

Off they went at the quick; then, with a wild cheer, broke into a loping run, the extremities of the semicircle closing in as they advanced.

The shark-charmer ran towards the Elephant's head, where the precipice was the loftiest and dizziest of the four, the beach lying full three hundred feet below. Whatever chance of escape he possessed, it assuredly did not lie in that direction. To all human seeming his escape was an utter impossibility. So thought the *peons*, and slackened speed, though the extremities of the living, steel-crested semicircle still closed in and in. Between, and somewhat ahead, ran the shark-charmer. He could not run much farther; the brink of the precipice was only a few yards away. He was caught!

What the thoughts of the guilty, hunted wretch were during those awful moments, God alone knows.

The *peons* had slowed down to a walk now—a walk confident, yet timid. They were altogether sure of the shark-charmer, and not a little afraid of the precipice. Not so the fugitive; for him all fear lay behind. He advanced to the very brink of the cliff. His arms dropped at his sides.

In upon him closed his pursuers with cat-like tread and alert eyes. They had no desire to be dashed over the cliff. Besides, was he not as good as caught? A mere span of rock divided him from their grasp. He stood motionless, half-turned towards them, apparently resigned to his fate.

Suddenly, however, hurling upon the close-drawn ranks a swift look of defiance, he wheeled full-face to the sea; wheeled, and drew his arms up and back.

Captain Leigh was the first to perceive the significance of the movement.

"Seize him!" he shouted, dashing through the line of *peons*; "quick, or he'll be over!... Good God!"

He fell back appalled. A stifled cry of horror broke from the *peons*. The shark-charmer had leapt into mid-air.

CHAPTER XXVI.

BRINGS THE QUEST TO AN END.

SILENT and pale as death, Don turned and stood for a moment facing Haunted Pagoda Hill, with head bared. His thoughts were with the captain as he had seen him on that terrible evening of the murder. Plainer than words his attitude cried:

"Avenged!"

The other natives had taken advantage of the opportunity afforded by the pursuit of the shark-charmer to make good their escape. Captain Leigh accordingly ordered the *peons* back to the schooner. Their mission was at an end.

At the head of the stairs they came upon Bosin. The monkey at once clambered on to Don's shoulder, happier far than his new master.

Here, too, as they were about to turn their backs upon the spot where death had hovered in ever-narrowing circles about their heads through the hopeless hours of that awful night and day, Jack and Don joined hands and silently renewed the friendship which had here been put to so crucial a test. Our boy-friendships seldom pass the boundary line of youth and manhood; or, if they do, too often become tarnished and neglected things in which we find no pleasure. Theirs, just then, seemed fit to last a lifetime.

"Say!" cried Jack abruptly, when he had done wringing his chum's hand, "what about the pearls, old fellow? You're surely not going off without them after all the trouble we've had? I'm not, anyhow!"

Jack was nothing if not practical.

Captain Leigh, who was standing by, overheard the words, and approached with a curious, not to say mysterious, smile on his lips.

"What! not had enough of it yet, Jack?" said he, in bantering tones.

"Not I, sir! Where's the use of being half cut to bits if one doesn't get what one's after? I shan't be content till I handle the shiners."

"And where do you purpose looking for them?"

Jack's face fell. It was not easy to find an answer to this question.

T

"Perhaps I can assist you," continued Captain Leigh, with a repetition of his mysterious smile. "This quest of yours, boys, has been a string of surprises from the very start, judging by what I have heard and seen of it. So, just to keep the ball rolling, we'll wind up with the biggest surprise of all."

And slipping his fingers into his waistcoat pocket, to the astonishment of the young men he drew therefrom the identical wash-leather case which they had all along, and with good reason, supposed to be in the shark-charmer's possession.

"Why—how—?" Don began, hardly able to believe his eyes.

Jack interrupted him.

"Don't you see how it is?" cried he. "The governor's running a rig on us. Old Salambo took the pearls, but left the bag; it's empty, of course!"

Captain Leigh quietly turned the pouch upside-down, and poured into the palm of his left hand a little silvery heap with a shimmer of pale gold in its midst. This he pushed into full view with his finger. It was the Golden Pearl.

"You don't mean to say we've been on a wild-goose chase all this time?" gasped Jack.

"A downright fool's errand!" muttered Don, in tones of intense disgust.

"No; neither one nor the other," interposed Captain Leigh. "Don't go scattering self-accusations of that sort about before you hear my explanation — though it's a queer business, I must acknowledge," he added, with a laugh. "Will you hear it out now or wait till we go on board?"

"Tell us one thing," put in Don; "were the pearls stolen at all?"

"No, they were not, or I should not be able to produce them. But the shark-charmer was none the less a thief, for all that. But I see you're on tenterhooks to hear all about it, so I'll read you the riddle at once."

Carefully restoring the pearls to the pouch, he handed the treasure to Don, and then resumed:

"It goes without saying, of course, that you remember the evening you brought the pearls on board. Well, shortly after you had placed them in the locker—you had just turned in, I think— I got an uneasy sort of feeling that they were not as safe there as they should be——"

"So you took them into your state-room!"

interrupted Don, who thought he began to see light.

"Exactly. The companion door was open, you recollect, and the shark-charmer, I suppose, must have been hanging about at the moment and seen me. Very imprudently, as it turned out, I left my door on the latch, though I took the precaution to put the pearls under my pillow. You remember, perhaps, my paying off some of the men that afternoon? Well, when I turned in I left the bag of rupees—or rather what remained of them, about two hundred in all, I should think—on the sofa opposite my berth, and my gold chronometer on the stand at my head, as I always do. I slept like a top until I was called at three, when we got under weigh. At this time, you understand, I was under the impression that you two were snug between the sheets. The schooner was a dozen miles down the coast before I found out my mistake. Being due in Colombo the following day, you see, I couldn't put back. Neither could I make head nor tail of your disappearance until the carrier brought your letter, Don. That made the whole matter plain enough. You had found the locker empty, supposed that the shark-charmer had stolen the pearls, and had given chase."

"Then," cried Jack, "what I said a minute ago was right enough, after all. The pearls were safe, and we've been on a jolly wild-goose chase."

"Oh, no; that doesn't follow. The shark-charmer left the schooner far from empty-handed. He stole the bag of rupees and the watch."

"Ah, but what about the handkerchief the pearls were tied up in?" asked Don. "I fished it out of the water off the island here. How do you account for that?"

"I must have thrown the handkerchief on the sofa. Probably the fellow snatched it up with the bag of rupees, thinking that it still contained the pearls."

"And threw it away when he found that it didn't," chuckled Jack. "Well, the shiners are all right, anyhow!"

Nightfall found the schooner bowling towards the open sea under full sail. Three figures stood grouped on her deck in the fading twilight.

"It was just about here," said Don in a choked voice :

> "Here, a sheer hulk, lies poor Tom Bowling,
>   The darling of our crew;
> No more he'll hear the tempest howling,
>   For death has broached him to.

> His form was of the manliest beauty,
> His heart was kind and soft;
> Faithful below he did his duty,
> But now he's gone aloft."

All three uncovered and stood with bowed heads until the old sailor's resting-place was left far behind.

THE END.

F. M. EVANS AND CO., LIMITED, PRINTERS, CRYSTAL PALACE, S.E.

www.ingramcontent.com/pod-product-compliance
Lightning Source LLC
Chambersburg PA
CBHW032103230426
43672CB00009B/1626